CAREERS in

HIGH TECH

DISCARD

Professional Careers Series

HIGH TECH

NICHOLAS BASTA

THIRD EDITION

New York   Chicago   San Francisco   Lisbon   London   Madrid   Mexico City
Milan   New Delhi   San Juan   Seoul   Singapore   Sydney   Toronto

The McGraw·Hill Companies

Library of Congress Cataloging-in-Publication Data

Basta, Nicholas, 1954–
    Careers in high tech / Nicholas Basta.—3rd ed.
      p. cm.
    ISBN 0-07-147612-1 (alk. paper)
    1. Engineering—Vocational guidance.   2. Scientists—Vocational guidance.
  3. Technologists—Vocational guidance.   I. Title.

  TA157.B3418   2007
  620.0023—dc22   2006028912

1 2 3 4 5 6 7 8 9 0   DOC/DOC   10 9 8 7

ISBN-13: 978-0-07-147612-6
ISBN-10:   0-07-147612-1

McGraw-Hill books are available at special quantity discounts to use as premiums and
sales promotions, or for use in corporate training programs. For more information, please
write to the Director of Special Sales, Professional Publishing, McGraw-Hill, Two Penn
Plaza, New York, NY 10121-2298. Or contact your local bookstore.
This book is printed on acid-free paper.

The information contained in this book is intended to provide helpful and informative
material on the subject addressed. It is not intended to serve as a replacement for
professional medical advice. A health-care professional should be consulted regarding
your specific situation.

This book is printed on acid-free paper.

CONTENTS

HIGH TECH

PART

ONE

The High-Tech Professions

High-tech companies often have odd names, usually with *X, -tech, -tex,* or *-gen* in their label. They have futuristic-looking headquarters buildings, often designed and constructed by the company executives and sometimes located in remote, scenic parts of North America such as New Hampshire, Oregon, or British Columbia. Their executives may drive Ferraris or Jaguars into the company parking lot—or may commute via bicycle. Usually these executives have a hard time describing to outsiders what the company does.

Who are these companies? Because of the variety of businesses they are in, ranging from medicine to energy to electronics, they are hard to unify under one umbrella. Wall Street analysts, wanting to make life simple by doing just that, have called them high technology or high-tech companies. They are revolutionizing industry, and their products are changing our lives.

That description of high tech needs emphasis. There is no formal definition of high technology, as opposed to low or any other form of technology. (There is a classification of industries as high, medium, and low tech, but not a classification of specific technologies. See Chapter 2.) Many people believe that high technology refers only to the wonders of computers, software, and electronics—information technology (IT). They are not wrong, but they are unintentionally limiting the scope of the field. Anywhere you look at electronics, you inevitably find some connection to another area of science. Computers, for example, depend heavily on data storage systems, and those systems depend on mechanical disks (such as the hard drive in the computer you might be using) that are the invention of highly specialized materials scientists who develop the disk materials and read/write mechanisms. Is the electronics engineer who designed the computer a high-tech worker, and the materials scientist a low-tech worker? The answer is no. They are both working on high-tech applications.

A professional development specialist, representing one of the largest scientific societies in the world, exemplified this confusion when contacted for this book. "Our members are not high-tech workers," she asserted. But when it was pointed out that the members of her professional society are researching revolutionary technologies in biomaterials, sophisticated databases, nanomaterials, and energy generation, she agreed that indeed there are high-tech workers in the profession.

For a generation, high-tech companies have garnered the spotlight in business circles. There is a well-established pattern of new scientific discoveries leaving the academic laboratory, incubating at small, privately funded research companies, and then, if the new idea makes sense commercially, growing into major corporations almost in the blink of an eye. The list of companies is long and is growing longer each year. Today, the buzz is with Internet companies like Google, Yahoo! and eBay. A decade earlier, the focus was on computer companies like Apple, Cisco, or Sun Microsystems. In biotechnology, what were small laboratories in the 1980s have grown to be pharmaceutical powerhouses: Amgen, Genentech, Biogen Idec. In electronics, the leaders are Intel, Motorola, and Texas Instruments. Standing behind the smaller research firms are some mighty industrial giants that were themselves the entrepreneurially driven high-tech firms of previous generations. These include Xerox, IBM, Hewlett-Packard, Exxon, Merck, Dow Chemical, DuPont, Boeing, and General Motors.

The small entrepreneurial companies that are the source of many technological innovations are the heart of high tech. But it is very much the nature of high tech that it influences all sorts of low-tech or "no-tech" fields. Think of the sophisticated computers and software that are being used today to create animated movies. Animation is something that had been done manually for nearly a century; now it is an exciting, fast-changing part of the movie business. Another example is the process of making a mock-up or model of a new clothing style, automobile body, or mechanical part. Craftspeople used to work long hours to create these models out of cloth, clay, or paper; now a computer-driven, laser-powered device can make many of them without human intervention, working from a design that was itself sketched out on a computer.

So, if high technology is not limited to electronics or computers, and if it can be applied to mundane applications as well as advanced ones, what is it? I would suggest that it simply represents the leading edge of applied scientific research at any given time. The key words here are *leading edge* and *applied*. Leading edge simply means wherever the scientific research is at the forefront, leading to new discoveries and new inventions. *Applied* in this context means science for daily use in society and business. We are not, for example, talking about the leading research in paleontology, no matter how exciting the discovery of a new dinosaur might be. We are talking about products that are part of activities we are engaged in every day, such as using telecommunications systems, getting a CAT scan as part of a checkup, or playing the latest video game. In the early days of computer display technology, believe it or not, playing tic-tac-toe was a high-tech innovation; now it is a historical artifact. In the early days of telephony, you cranked a local telephone machine to be connected to an operator, who then manually connected you to another party. Today it's all done in milliseconds by very high-tech digital switches.

Think of this book as a ticket to a roller-coaster ride through high technology. The sights and sounds are dazzling and a little scary. High technology can certainly be intimidating to think about as a place in which to find a career. But relatively few people set up their entire careers in advance. Most people who end up in high-tech careers, having discovered that they are fairly good at math or science as students, decide to study science or engineering in college. Once they graduate, they find people and companies working in exciting new fields, and they want to participate. They obtain a job and begin pitching in with contributions on how a technology should be developed or applied. These workers can then go in many different directions—teaching the use of the new technology to customers or to students, selling the technology to buyers, helping manufacture a product, helping install or service the product, or writing about the product so users know how it works. If a worker is successful in these endeavors, he or she may rise in the management of the company, becoming an administrator who may not ever write computer code or touch a laboratory beaker but who guides the efforts of other high-tech workers.

Thus, to have a career in high tech it is not essential to be the world's sharpest scientist in some area of technology. What is most essential is to be eternally curious about how things work (or should work) and to be willing to learn continuously. Some high-tech researchers stop working after five or so years and go back to school to learn a new area of science or technology. All of them must seek to continually educate themselves to keep up with the advances in their field of technology.

It is this curiosity and willingness to learn that distinguishes the high-tech worker from most others. In many other professions workers learn a skill in college or immediately after graduation and spend the rest of their careers refining that skill and gaining experience in using it. That's not bad, and many people enjoy the chance to do one thing especially well. But that's not the outlook of the high-tech worker. "You shouldn't just keep getting to be better and better" at one type of work, a career counselor was quoted as saying in *Business Week*. "You need a diversity of skills in your career portfolio. The more you have, the more marketable you are."

CHAPTER

1

TECHNOLOGY AND SCIENCE

Science is something that you probably have become familiar with during various high school courses. Science is the body of knowledge that addresses what the physical universe is made of and how it functions. In the history of science dating back more than three thousand years, science and philosophy (the study of all types of knowledge) were intertwined. Ancient Greek philosophers, for example, attempted to explain the motions of the planets or the variety of living things strictly through mental exercises. Conversely, they reasoned through moral and religious issues by looking at the natural world around them.

Starting around 1600 and becoming widespread in Europe during the 1700s, a new concept of science arose. Science became the practice of examining and proving the unknown through experimentation. If you could conduct an experiment to prove the presence of, say, metal in soil, then you would make a contribution to the body of scientific knowledge. If you could not conceive of an experiment that would answer such a question, then the question was not one that could properly be addressed by science. (Questions that are not properly addressed by science are the sphere of religion, morality, and philosophy.)

WHAT IS TECHNOLOGY?

Science addresses fundamental questions about the universe, such as how matter and energy combine or what the fundamental particles of material things are. By studying such things, scientists hope to gain a better understanding of the universe. Once this understanding has been achieved, it can be applied to improve human conditions—and this is where technology comes in. Technologists take the new knowledge that scientists have uncovered and seek to apply it in ways that are useful to humanity.

A close reading of the history of technology reveals that many technological achievements, such as innovations in agriculture or medicine, took place before the foundations of formal scientific research were built. Around the 1700s, the technological advances occurring in industry merged with the scientific advances occurring among researchers, and the two have been intertwined ever since.

Technology surrounds us from the moment we wake up until we fall asleep and has made possible the comfortable lifestyles many of us enjoy. Technology has also created many of the ills our society faces today, from such environmental catastrophes as the depletion of the ozone layer to the harmful effects of television on the education of the young. Some people believe that our technology is the culmination of four thousand years of human advancement, enabling us to travel to the stars or live under the oceans. Others believe that technology is an inhuman force, pushing humanity in directions that it would not go by choice.

Technology is neither as great a force as some believe nor as beneficial as some of its proponents claim. Many thinkers have sought to resolve questions about the usefulness of technology in recent years.

One of the best analyses of technology came from Samuel Florman, a civil engineer in the New York area, who wrote a classic book, *The Existential Pleasures of Engineering*, in 1976 (St. Martin's Press). In it, Florman argues that technology cannot be the unstoppable force that some people think it is simply because it so often fails. Every year thousands of new products are offered to the consumer; the majority of these fail to sell well within that year. Those failures imply that the everyday consumer still can choose among a variety of options, and the technological option is only one of them. While new types of technology are continually being offered to the public, only those that meet a desired end succeed commercially. Technological success often does not translate into commercial success.

Conversely, there have been many technologies that have changed our lives immeasurably. The telephone, electricity, and the railroad were the technological marvels of the nineteenth century; the automobile, television, and the personal computer revolutionized twentieth-century life.

The early years of this century have been dominated by the Internet and similar communications technologies.

WHO WORKS IN TECHNOLOGY?

While it takes individual consumers to make a technology succeed, it takes inventors and innovators to dream up the technology to begin with. The choices you make in what subjects to study and what industries to join will shape the future course of technology. Here the personal issue of science versus technology comes to the fore. Most professional scientists (those with a doctoral degree) are engaged in research and development (R&D). Many of them work on college campuses; others work in the R&D labs of private firms or large corporations.

The workday of such professional scientists is not too far from the experiences you may have had in high school science laboratories. The experiment is the crucial learning mechanism for these workers. R&D scientists run experiments, analyze the results, and share those results with other scientists to arrive at theories of why the experiments came out the way they did.

Engineers and industrial technology graduates typically do not work in laboratories. They work at factories, in design offices, or in the field, taking measurements of, say, the chemical purity of underground water and then seeking useful applications of those measurements. In this specific case, the goal may be to find a new source of drinkable water or to track pollutants moving through the ground. Then they will use knowledge gained from textbooks or studies that scientists have written to determine the proper course of action. Sometimes the necessary scientific knowledge for a precise analysis of a situation is lacking; in such cases, engineers know how to conduct their own experiments to derive a general path for going forward in development.

In fact, it is quite frequently the case that some knotty technological problem eventually leads to new scientific knowledge. Scientists hear about a problem from engineers or other technologically oriented workers and then try to reason through the fundamental facts that would explain or answer the problem. One example of this is the current push among semi-conductor chip manufacturers to shrink their devices into the submicron level (a micron is a millionth of a meter; a human hair is about 100 microns thick). As electronics design engineers create smaller circuits, new atomic-level effects, known as quantum tunneling, occur. These quantum effects were first theorized by atomic physicists in the first half of the twentieth century. Today's physicists are revisiting the topic, finding ways to use quantum tunneling and other atomic effects usefully in the next generation of microelectronics.

There are, of course, scientists who work primarily outside the laboratory—even on the factory floor—and engineers who work exclusively in laboratories. Generally speaking, any engineer or scientist with a doctoral degree (Ph.D.) is a candidate for laboratory research. Scientists and engineers with master's or bachelor's degrees perform various functions in a variety of settings:

1. At manufacturers these high-tech workers are involved in production, design, quality control, testing, and management.
2. At consulting firms (which typically have manufacturing clients) they work as designers and specifiers. The most common form of consulting is construction services: for example, designing and then building a skyscraper or highway.
3. In the services sector of the economy, such as banking, communications, or transportation, engineers and scientists provide specialized advice and consultation. For a bank, for example, electrical engineers and computer scientists may work to design and install a combined computing and communications network.
4. In government, engineers and scientists provide a diverse array of services. Some work as researchers in the network of national laboratories, performing experiments just as a researcher at a private company or a university would. A large number perform military research for vehicles, weapons, or defensive systems. Others act as administrators or program directors, guiding the efforts of other scientists. Still others are involved in the regulation of commerce, such as establishing standards for communications, foods and drugs, environmental performance, and health and safety.

A few words about nontechnical professions and their place in the high-tech world: while it is clear that mathematical or scientific prowess is the distinctive feature of high-tech workers, many types of professionals work in high-tech industries. A high-tech company needs lawyers, human resources managers, accountants, marketing and sales executives, and more. One type of career path, which will be described in more detail later in this book, involves starting in a technical specialty and then moving over the course of one's career into business management, sales, or other non-technical lines of work. It is also quite common for nontechnical college graduates to assume these types of work. There is an advantage for such nontechnical professionals to have at least an affinity for high-tech knowledge—the ability and willingness to talk tech with scientists or engineers. There are numerous stories about high-tech companies being run by nontechnical managers; those executives have had to learn to deal with technology, even if they themselves do not develop technology. Like any other type of business, high-tech companies need a wide range of skills to be successful.

One other category of nontechnical professional can be essential to many high-tech companies: the creative designer or artist. The movie animators mentioned earlier are just one type of work where creative artistry is valued. New-style Internet companies need designers who understand human interaction with screens, sounds, and other media to be successful. An evolving field, industrial product design calls for all sorts of creative input from artists, psychologists, teachers, writers, and others. These creative workers sometimes have a technical background and sometimes don't, but all of them need to have an understanding of how technological features translate into consumer benefits.

STATISTICS ON THE PROFESSIONS

All high-tech workers deal with numbers—so let's look at some numbers that sum up this information. For the United States, the Bureau of Labor Statistics (BLS) provides detailed assessments of the numbers of workers with various types of occupations in its Occupational Projections and Training Data. The listing is comprehensive, covering 250 occupations ranging from government chief executives to parking lot attendants, from nuclear engineers to dancers. Table 1.1 provides a count of the professions most closely related to high-tech work. The BLS also uses economic projections to make an estimate of future job growth in these occupations (column 3) and gives the results of salary surveys for each occupation (column 5).

Some high-tech jobs show the strongest projected growth rates of any occupation—50 percent or more. Others are only average or below average, which would normally indicate a line of work with poor job prospects. However, one has to be careful not to read too much into this data. The nature of much high-tech work is to create a business, and jobs, that didn't exist before. It is not possible to predict events like this with economic or employment projections. The BLS projections are valuable for showing where an existing technology—which might be quite new—is rapidly creating new employment opportunities. More so than most professions, however, high-tech workers create their own opportunities.

A June 2005 survey for the Software Human Resource Council of Canada (SHRC), looking specifically at current job demand for IT professionals, found that the highest ranked categories were for personal computer operating systems, Internet-based networking, and data security technologies ("Outlook for 2005: Re-Investment and Rationalization: The Leading IT Skills in Demand within Canadian Organizations in 2005," accessed at shrc.ca, May 2006). The organization also looked at trends in engineering and computer-based academic enrollments and, in an April 2005 report ("University Engineering Enrollment Survey: A Summary of the Findings") found that engineering enrollments are projected to be up by around 10 percent over the 2002 to 2006 period, but that IT-related disciplines (computer engineering, software engineering, computer science) were projected to decline by as much as 22 percent. Canada had its own Internet dot-com bust in the period from 2001 to 2003, and various press reports say that as many as one hundred thousand IT jobs were lost during the period. But rising employment has more than made up for those losses, and indeed, most displaced workers were able to find other IT-related jobs. The overall picture seems to be that today's Canadian college students are reacting to recent history in the Canadian high-tech industries, rather than projecting future trends.

WHERE DO TECHNOLOGISTS WORK?

The question of location has two factors: the workplaces of technologists across North America and the trends in location of technology work internationally. As we'll see, these two factors are intertwined.

Table 1.1 U.S. Occupational Projections, 2004–2014*

Occupations	Employment, in Thousands		Percent Change	2004 Median Annual Earnings, in Dollars
	2004	**2014**		
Network systems analysts	231	357	54.6	60,600
Computer software engineers, applications	460	682	48.4	74,980
Computer software engineers, systems	340	486	43.0	79,740
Medical scientists	77	103	34.0	54,800–61,320
Computer systems analysts	487	640	31.4	66,460
Biomedical engineers	10	13	30.7	67,690
Environmental engineers	49	64	30.6	66,480
Computer and information systems managers	280	353	26.0	92,570
Computer and information scientists, research	22	28	25.6	85,190
Environmental scientists and geoscientists	109	126	17.0	51,080–80,150
Biological scientists	77	90	17.0	50,330–68,950
Civil engineers	237	276	16.5	64,230
Science technicians	342	391	14.4	29,730–40,260
All engineers	1,449	1,643	13.4	
TOTAL, ALL OCCUPATIONS	**145,612**	**154,540**	**13.0**	
Engineers, managers	190	215	13.0	97,630
Materials engineers	21	24	12.2	67,110
All physical scientists	250	281	12.2	56,060–97,320
Electrical engineers	156	174	11.8	71,610
Mechanical engineers	226	251	11.1	66,320
Chemical engineers	31	34	10.6	76,770
Computer hardware engineers	77	84	10.1	64,230
Electrical and electronic engineering technicians	182	199	9.8	46,310
Electronics engineers	143	157	9.7	75,770
Mathematical sciences	107	117	9.7	58,620–81,240

(Continued)

Table 1.1 U.S. Occupational Projections, 2004–2014* (*Continued*)

Occupations	Employment, in Thousands		Percent Change	2004 Median Annual Earnings, in Dollars
	2004	2014		
Aerospace engineers	76	82	8.3	79,100
Materials scientists	8	8	8.0	72,390
Chemists	82	88	7.3	56,060
Physicists	15	16	7.0	87,450
Computer programmers	455	464	2.0	62,890

*High-tech occupations are ranked by highest average growth to lowest according to column 4, "percent change" in employment, 2004–2014. Average growth for all occupations in the U.S. workforce is indicated by the "Total, All Occupations" listing at the middle of the table. Job titles above this entry have *higher than average* growth, while those below it have *lower than average* growth.

Source: U.S. Bureau of Labor Statistics

The workplaces of high-tech employees vary considerably. They are frequently in laboratories, especially if the employees are doing scientific research. The laboratories, in turn, might be located on college campuses, at corporate R&D centers, or in government facilities. Because so much technology is applied to manufacturing, high-tech workers are also located at factories, but the great majority of them do not actually work in a factory. As so much high-tech work involves careful analysis of data, experiments, or literature searching, the work tends to be in office buildings that might or might not be near the factory.

Other types of high-tech employment take the worker out of the office. For many complex information-technology projects, workers must be at the site of a client organization where a new system is being installed. Some of these projects can be so extensive and lengthy that the workers have their own offices on the client's site. In other cases, the worker drives out to the client location, performs a task over the course of several hours, and then leaves. Some high-tech work, of its very nature, must occur in the field. Using sophisticated visual mapping devices for a construction site, for example, requires the worker to be at the site. Performing studies of bioengineered agricultural materials could require lengthy trips through farms. These types of tasks can take the high-tech worker literally all over the world.

There is a distinct geography to high tech. Everyone has heard, by now, of Silicon Valley, the grouping of microelectronics companies that began in northern California during the 1960s and grew to be an economic powerhouse of discovery, innovation, and business success in the succeeding decades. Silicon Valley is the best example of a trend in economic development that has grown more diverse in recent years. Silicon Valley got started when two engineers at Stanford University started a business literally in their own garage; that company became Hewlett-Packard. Its continuing development depended on steady interaction with the laboratories of Stanford, and as the company grew, it became a ready source of employment for Stanford grads. Soon other companies took advantage of the same combination of research centers, trained workers, and economic incentives from the university, the region, and the state. The pattern has been repeated in locations including Austin, Texas, and Research Triangle Park, North Carolina. In some locations, a grouping of hospitals and health-care centers has led to a concentration of medical research industries, as in Houston, St. Louis, and New York. Canada has numerous information technology organizations centered around Toronto.

At this point, most large urban centers with at least a handful of universities attract new companies, much as seedlings grow in the vicinity of a mature tree. Some regions have formalized this process with incubator facilities designed to expedite the conversion of academic research into industrial innovation. In sum, high-tech workers tend to congregate where high-tech research is performed.

Along the way, however, high tech itself has changed the practice of high-tech work. New communications capabilities enable remote offices to perform work as if all the workers were in the same location. This capability has led to what is called, in business circles, *outsourcing*. Outsourcing means that certain business functions can be performed by an outside company as a service. In the early years of outsourcing, only very routine tasks, such as compiling payroll data or billing, were outsourced. Soon innovative companies found that they could hand off most if not all of their IT work to the outside company, including the installation of completely new software systems to run the company. Data simply flows back and forth from the client company to the outsourced IT provider.

The next iteration of this process, which became fairly prominent at the turn of this century, was to outsource the IT and related work to a company in another country, especially emerging nations like India, Indonesia, and China. These countries have large numbers of well-trained engineers and computer programmers who can be hired at dramatically lower rates of pay than North American workers. The result: a sizeable amount of IT and related work has been not only outsourced, but offshored. The practice has generated more than a little controversy as complaints arise that U.S. employers are exporting jobs to other countries. But the reality is that most large multinational companies compete on a global scale and will shuffle projects and resources as best they can to cut costs and win business. Many North American students believe that as a result of these practices, engineering or IT jobs are not worth pursuing. But the reality is that the amount of technical work is rising on a global scale. There are as many opportunities for well-educated engineers, IT workers, and scientists with bright ideas as ever. The most that can be said is that like few other professions, high-tech workers have a global arena of opportunities.

WHAT IS HIGH TECHNOLOGY?

THINKING OUTSIDE THE BOX

Most people think of high technology as something to do with computers and electronics. Those two industries are very much part of the high-tech landscape, but after those two, there is very little consensus over what else is high tech. Biotechnology—the manipulation of genetic material to develop new drugs or diagnostic techniques—is often mentioned, but biotechnology is only a part of the pharmaceutical industry, so let's include pharmaceuticals as well. Lasers—a special type of light that is powerful enough to cut through metal—are also often thought of as high tech, but the largest use of lasers today is in telecommunications, which includes the telephone, satellites, radio, television, cable TV, and so forth. Those industries should be added to the list, too.

You may have heard recently about nanomaterials—particles with a specified shape, but that are measured in millionths of a meter (microns). Nanomaterials, some of which are already commercialized, are being proposed for new types of microelectronics, for stronger-than-steel structural materials, and for microscopic medical devices that would wander around one's body, fighting disease. Nanotech is now well on its way to being a high-tech industry.

Today's high gasoline and petroleum prices have reawakened efforts to create alternative fuels, ranging from the hydrogen-powered car that was promoted during the first George W. Bush administration to fuel cells (which might, interestingly, be based on nanomaterials), solar power, and fuels based on the conversion of biomass. Mention of fuels inevitably loops into the pressing problem of global warming, which will be addressed by developing energy sources that do not depend on fossil fuels. A host of tangled scientific and technological issues, ranging from computer-based global weather modeling to a potential rebirth of nuclear energy, will be examined as solutions to the problem.

Looking in another direction—that of medicine—we are now entering an era of personalized medicine arising from the enumeration of the human genome. There was a near-decade-long race, ending in 2003, to read out the entire genetic string that makes up human DNA. Out of three billion nucleotide bases (individual genetic building blocks), there are an estimated 1.4 million single nucleotide polymorphisms, known as SNPs (pronounced "snips"), that vary from person to person. Within this category can be found the variations that make one individual different from the next, including such factors as a predisposition to certain diseases. Today there is a growing battery of genetic tests that identify susceptibilities to certain diseases or reactions to certain drugs. Tomorrow there will be medications designed specifically for an individual's genetic structure. This points to entirely new methods of analyzing patients' health, of manufacturing medications, and of how these medications are delivered to the patient.

A similar prospect follows from recent work on stem cells, which are the starting cells out of which the many specialized cells and organs of the human body originate. The field has some controversy because of its dependence on human embryonic cells, but is likely to proceed in a variety of pathways. There are, for example, stem cells even in adults; it may ultimately turn out that a person's own stem cells can be used for treating that individual. Stem cell science is being proposed for a wide range of conditions, from genetic diseases, to repairing spinal cords so paraplegics can regain use of their limbs, to replacing entire organs. A worldwide race is on to explore this science and develop usable medical techniques.

Finally, there are the age-old problems of humanity, against which scientists and technologists have struggled for millennia. They include widespread disease, world hunger, the need for clean water, and education. Addressing these problems requires an international commitment—a good example of this was the program, over the course of a couple of decades, to eradicate the smallpox virus. Successful programs are not magically created by some technological wave of the hand, but new technology definitely has a place in speeding along the resolution of these problems.

As described in the Part One overview, the term *high technology* arose from government agencies and Wall Street investors seeking to distinguish science-driven businesses from those that have other drivers. The Organisation of Economic Cooperation and Development (OECD), an agency of the European Union, developed a system of categorizing industries by their research intensity, that is, the amount of money the companies in that industry spend on R&D relative to their overall expenses, and found that two groupings spent significantly more on R&D than others (see Table 2.1).

Table 2.1 OECD's Ranking of U.S. High-Tech Industries

Rank / Industry	R&D Intensity
1. Office, accounting, and computing machinery	14.7
2. Aircraft and spacecraft	14.6
3. Pharmaceuticals	12.4
4. Radio, television, and communication equipment	8.6
5. Medical, precision, and optical instruments	7.9

Some medium-tech industries include chemicals, motor vehicles, and electrical machinery; some low-tech industries include petroleum refining, shipbuilding, and metal refining. Although accurate as far as it goes, this OECD ranking illustrates the problem of identifying high tech as part of a national economy: "office, accounting, and computing machinery" does not get one thinking about high-end game consoles; "precision instruments" does not conjure up images of robots or nanoscale switches. Even high-tech industries as categorized this way contain a lot of humdrum products and business activities. Moreover, with a little head scratching, it's not hard to think of high-tech developments in low-tech industries—for example, using genetically engineered microbes to refine metals out of low-grade ores, or high-efficiency lightbulbs that use advanced light-emitting polymers in place of incandescent wires (these are actual R&D projects these days).

CHARACTERISTICS OF HIGH-TECH INDUSTRIES

It could be more insightful, especially from a career-planning perspective, to think of the common elements of high technology regardless of the industry it is being deployed in. There are at least four elements common to high-tech developments, which we will examine in turn.

Innovations Based on Scientific and Engineering Research

First, high technology is the fruit of scientific and engineering research. This simply means that scientists and engineers are the inventors or developers of the innovations. In the business world, thousands of new products or ways of doing things are invented each year. A bank, for example, might innovate by offering a new savings plan for depositors. A restaurant might innovate by devising a new type of cuisine. These developments are indeed new, but they are not technical in nature. (They may, however, be as profitable to the company offering them as any high-tech product.) So, obviously, high technology involves the use of technology.

Radically New Ways of Doing Things

Second, high technology is radically new. Many companies employ scientists, engineers, and other professionals to make improvements or modifications to existing products. A chemical company, for example, might find a way to make a plastic without wasting any of the raw materials. An aerospace manufacturer might improve the fuel efficiency of its aircraft by adapting engine modifications. These developments are technical in nature, but they are only an extension of existing practices. However, when a computer company performs research on a parallel processing supercomputer (this term will be explained later), that represents something very new to the field. That makes it high technology.

Commercial Applications

The third point, that the innovation is commercial, is what distinguishes pure from applied scientific research. These two terms have traditionally indicated the separation between scientific research that is performed for its own sake, as a way of increasing the knowledge of humanity, and that which is done in order to make money. Examples of pure scientific research can be found in astronomy, where scientists study how the stars evolve or whether there are other planets in the galaxy. Another example is in mathematics, where scientists examine logical ways to manipulate numbers and other symbols, usually simply for the joy of being able to do so.

The funny thing about most types of pure research is that over time, discoveries that pure scientists make become something very useful to the applied scientists who are looking to solve everyday problems. To cite just one example, scientists in the 1930s and 1940s developed particle accelerators—machines that could speed up atomic particles and ram them into each other—as a way to study atomic physics. By the 1970s and 1980s these types of machines were being used to build microelectronic components; now they are being talked about as a way to cure cancer. Neither of these results was remotely thought of when scientists first devised the accelerators. They simply wanted to look more deeply into the atom. But the knowledge gained by those original scientists was found to be incredibly useful to later generations of researchers.

Another illustrative example shows up in the 2006 American Competitiveness Initiative, an effort by the Bush administration to renew the United States' success in commercializing technology. The authors of the report looked at the wildly popular Apple iPod music player, which was commercialized in 2004. Inside this deceptively simple device are a host of high-tech products:

1. **Very large scale integration (VLSI) microchips.** The central processing units of most of today's electronic products, which trace back to funding by the U.S. Defense Advanced Research Projects Agency (DARPA) in the 1960s.

2. **Fast fourier transform (FFT) signal processing.** Enables sound to be translated back and forth into digital data quickly; the basic research can be traced back to projects funded by the Department of Defense in the mid-1960s.

3. **Thin-film transistor liquid crystal displays (LCDs).** Arose from National Science Foundation funding (and others) in the late 1980s.

4. **Spintronics-based micro hard drives.** For memory storage, based on a principle called the giant magnetorestrictive effect; in the late 1980s the U.S. Department of Energy was involved in research on thin-film metallic surfaces that enable this effect.

5. **Lithium-ion batteries.** Based in part on 1990-era research funded by the U.S. Department of Energy's electrochemistry program.

It's worth pointing out that some of these technical developments occurred forty years before the iPod music player was marketed, and that most likely no one working on VLSI chips or LCDs was thinking at the time about a portable music player. Research tends to evolve like that; technical developments are pursued and then become, years later, part of the technology toolbox product developers use to create new products.

It used to be true that there was a sharp distinction between pure and applied research and that all applied research was built on what pure scientists had done before. That distinction—never universally true to begin with—is fading from today's scene. Many types of applied research uncover some intriguing new property that results in fundamental new science. And many scientists and engineers who work in what is considered to be pure research find very quickly that once they have developed some new type of scientific knowledge they are in an excellent position to apply it to commercial products. Many companies today employ scientists and engineers simply to explore new ideas, hoping that those new ideas will result in something that will eventually become useful. Many scientists who work on college campuses, where they teach as well as perform research, also have business relationships with high-tech companies. For this reason, people rarely talk about themselves anymore as pure or applied scientists.

Elements of Risk

There is a fourth element to high technology, having to do with its commercial aspects. High technology is inherently risky to the businesses that seek to use it and to the careers of the people who engage in it. A great number of new technologies that look extremely promising when first conceived never pan out. The company that invests in new technology can go bankrupt. The scientists and engineers, along with all the other company employees, can lose their jobs.

Don't let these facts scare you off from a high-tech career, however—many other occupations have similar risks. Moreover, it is rare these days for new workers to join a company and then spend their entire career at that company. More often, professionals such as high-tech workers move from one firm to another, gaining experience in a variety of industries. An academic posting at a college or university might also be a part of one's career.

TODAY'S HIGH-TECH LINEUP

Picking winning technologies for the next several years is a favorite sport of magazine editors, think tanks, and book writers. Every January brings a slew of forecasts or top ten lists for the coming year; it's fun reading.

The process gets a lot more serious when business and government managers need to sit down and figure out how to allocate precious research dollars where they will do the most good. For government offices like the National Science Foundation, the National Institute for Science and Technology, the National Institutes of Health, and others, the goal is to use taxpayer dollars effectively to meet social and economic goals. For businesses, the decision making can be critical to the ongoing success of the organization; especially in high tech, making the wrong bets on technologies can quickly kill a company.

The perspective is quite different for the individual researcher or, for that matter, for how you should think about high-tech careers. Most of the time, researchers and other high-tech workers make a decision to work in a particular arena of technology and then strive to find ways to make the technology scientifically or commercially successful. The individual high-tech worker needs to make decisions on whether he or she is more committed to a particular area of technology or to a type of industry where that technology (and, conceivably, many others) might be applied.

The career of James Fergason, a scientist who was centrally involved in the development of the liquid crystal display (LCD), is a great example of commitment to a single technology. Dr. Fergason worked from the early 1960s and for the rest of his career on LCDs; he started at Westinghouse Electric Co., pursuing applications for using liquid crystal polymers as temperature sensors. In the late 1960s, he became a researcher at Kent State University, where he started his own company, called International Liquid Crystal Co., in 1970. He has stayed with that company for more than twenty years, ultimately accumulating more than 150 patents in the field. In 2006, he was awarded the Lemelson-MIT Prize, a valuable award that honors achievement in invention.

The case for a contrasting career could be made with Steve Jobs, founder of Apple Computer Co. The first Apple personal computers were commercialized in the late 1970s. From Apple, Jobs founded a second computer company, tried to commercialize a new computer operating system, and then got involved in computer animation as an investor in Pixar Corp. Later, he returned to Apple, rejuvenated the company, and created the business environment that made the iPod such a hit product. While many things can be said about the success Jobs has had over the years, one clear point is that he looked at meeting consumers' needs through the use of technology; as different needs arose, he focused on different technologies and applications.

Where the forecasts of government agencies of new or important technologies and the business drivers of inventors or corporate managers intersect is where opportunities are created. New research depends on funding from government or private sources; the next step is to commercialize the technology, which calls for teams of high-tech workers. So one way to identify opportunities for a high-tech career is to study where the funding "bets" are being made by the agencies and corporations.

There is no one authority on technology forecasts; they come from many sources, including individuals. We'll offer several such lists here. There is much to learn from comparing them or from figuring out how to associate a source of forecasting with the ultimate success of the technologies that are chosen, but everyone needs to recognize that these lists are themselves moving targets—they get revised, sharpened, or changed year by year.

The following is an edited list of capability goals identified by the White House American Competitiveness Initiative in early 2006:

- World-class capability and capacity in nanofabrication and nanomanufacturing that will help transform current laboratory science into a broad range of new industrial applications for virtually every sector of commerce, including telecommunications, computing, electronics, health care, and national security
- Chemical, biological, optical, and electronic materials breakthroughs critical to cutting-edge research in nanotechnology, biotechnology, alternative energy, and the hydrogen economy through essential infrastructure such as the National Synchrotron Light Source II and the NIST Center for Neutron Research
- World-leading high-end computing capability (at the petascale) and capacity, coupled with advanced networking, to enable scientific advancement through modeling and simulation at unprecedented scale and complexity across a broad range of scientific disciplines and important to areas such as intelligent manufacturing, accurate weather and climate prediction, and design of safe and effective pharmaceuticals
- Overcoming technological barriers to the practical use of quantum information processing to revolutionize fields of secure communications, as well as quantum mechanics simulations used in physics, chemistry, biology, and materials science

- Overcoming technological barriers to efficient and economic use of hydrogen, nuclear, and solar energy through new basic research approaches in materials science
- Addressing gaps and needs in cyber security and information assurance to protect our IT-dependent economy from both deliberate and unintentional disruption, and to lead the world in intellectual property protection and control
- Improvement of sensor and detection capabilities that will result in world-leading automation and control technologies with a broad range of applications important to areas such as national security, health care, energy, and manufacturing
- Development of manufacturing standards for the supply chain to advance and accelerate the development and integration of more efficient production practices
- Accelerated work on advanced standards for new technologies (NIST)
- Advances in materials science and engineering to develop technologies and standards for improving structural performance during hazardous events such as earthquakes and hurricanes

Another government source is the U.S. Census Bureau, which assesses technologies that can affect the United States' relative competitive trade position. The bureau has identified ten leading edge technologies that are important to U.S. trade:

- **Biotechnology.** The medical and industrial application of advanced genetic research to the creation of drugs, hormones, and other therapeutic products for both agricultural and human uses.
- **Life science technologies.** The application of nonbiological scientific advances to medicine. For example, advances such as nuclear magnetic resonance imaging, echocardiography, and novel chemistry, coupled with new drug manufacturing techniques, have led to new products that help control or eradicate disease.
- **Optoelectronics.** The development of electronics and electronic components that emit or detect light, including optical scanners, optical disk players, solar cells, photosensitive semiconductors, and laser printers.

- **Information and communications.** The development of products that process increasing amounts of information in shorter periods of time, including fax machines, telephone switching apparatus, radar apparatus, communications satellites, central processing units, and peripheral units such as disk drives, control units, modems, and computer software.
- **Electronics.** The development of electronic components (other than optoelectronic components), including integrated circuits, multilayer printed circuit boards, and surface-mounted components, such as capacitors and resistors, that improve performance and capacity and, in many cases, reduce product size.
- **Flexible manufacturing.** The development of products for industrial automation, including robots, numerically controlled machine tools, and automated guided vehicles, that permit greater flexibility in the manufacturing process and reduce human intervention.
- **Advanced materials.** The development of materials, including semiconductor materials, optical fiber cable, and videodisks, that enhance the application of other advanced technologies.
- **Aerospace.** The development of aircraft technologies, such as most new military and civil airplanes, helicopters, spacecraft (communication satellites excepted), turbojet aircraft engines, flight simulators, and automatic pilots.
- **Weapons.** The development of technologies with military applications, including guided missiles, bombs, torpedoes, mines, missile and rocket launchers, and some firearms.
- **Nuclear technology.** The development of nuclear production apparatus, including nuclear reactors and parts, isotopic separation equipment, and fuel cartridges (nuclear medical equipment is listed under life science technologies).

Computer software can be considered an "eleventh" technology that is classified within the information and communications technology category by the Census Bureau.

Another list of innovative research areas, reviewed in the National Science Foundation's *Science and Engineering Indicators 2006* report, evaluates the targets of venture capital funds in recent years. This is where investors are "putting their money where their mouth is," expecting these areas to have the biggest payoff in eventually commercialized developments. The targets are not high technology per se, but as you'll see from a glance at the following list, they are dominated by high-tech developments.

Rank of Venture Capital Investments by Industry (2004)

1. Software and services
2. Medical and health
3. Communications
4. Internet-specific
5. Semiconductors and other electronics
6. Biotechnology
7. Other (nonspecific)
8. Computer hardware
9. Industrial and energy
10. Consumer-related

Source: National Science Board. 2006. *Science and Engineering Indicators 2006.* Vol. 1, Figure 6-32, p. 6-40.

THE RACE TO PATENTS

One more perspective on high tech rounds out the different ways of looking at it. Since high tech, as we've defined it, is based on innovation, it makes sense to look at the areas where the most patents are generated. A patent, as legally defined, gives a company the exclusive use of an innovation for a set number of years; after that period of time, anyone can use the innovation. Inventors apply for patents in the same way gold prospectors used to stake a claim to the site where they found the metal; since the prospector had the insight (and luck) to find the site, the economic benefit properly belonged to the prospector. Similarly, companies apply for patents from national governments so they can proceed to commercialize a discovery without fear of the knowledge being stolen by others.

Patents rarely have equal value, just as gold strikes might have enormous value, or very little. So the raw count of patents is not an exclusive measure of the value of innovation. But it is a good measure of how lively the pace of technological development is in a field, and that, in turn, is a hallmark of a high-tech industry. The following list shows the most active areas in the United States (in other countries, other areas are more active).

Fifteen Most Emphasized U.S. Patent Classes for U.S. Corporations

1. Business practice, data processing
2. Surgery; light, thermal, and electrical applications
3. Computers and digital processing systems
4. Data processing, file management
5. Surgery instruments
6. Data-processing software
7. Wells
8. Prostheses
9. (Digital) processing architectures
10. Input/output digital processing systems
11. Data processing, artificial intelligence
12. Analytical and immunological testing
13. Surgical medicators and receptors
14. Multicellular living organisms
15. Computer memory

Source: National Science Board. 2006. *Science and Engineering Indicators 2006.*
Vol. 1, Table 6-5, p. 6-31.

Several qualifiers are in order: in making this ranking, the U.S. Patent and Trademark Office excluded patents by individuals and governments; it is primarily a measure of corporations' patent activity. Also, there is considerable development of patentable innovations by U.S. companies abroad (where the relevant high-tech job would be), even though the patent might be filed in the United States; conversely, many non-U.S. companies have R&D centers in the United States, yet might file the patents in their home countries first.

What is interesting about the U.S. list is that, except for wells (which have to do with petroleum exploration, among other things), all of the leading patent classes are either in digital hardware and software or in medical or biotech areas. The United States is the world leader in both these categories; while it competes and succeeds in many other areas as well, those areas are shared by other countries.

CHAPTER 5

HIGH-TECH WORKERS

In the world of business and careers, it is very doubtful you will encounter someone whose job title is "high-tech worker." One reason for this is that high tech is a grouping of a variety of industries or professional activities. People will have a job title relevant to their particular industry or activity, and then secondarily consider themselves high-tech workers. Another is that high tech is not a separate field of study from other parts of science and technology, as discussed earlier. High tech is those parts of technological development that are at the leading edge of commercialization.

So, who are these mysterious high-tech workers? In the next few sections, we will look at how professional work is distinguished from other kinds of work; how job titles are categorized; and how science and technology are organized on college campuses. Along the way, you will get a sense of the types of jobs that exist in high technology, and you might find the ones that appeal to you very directly. However, keep in mind that high technology continually reinvents itself. If you have a vision of a particular kind of work, or a new idea, you will also invent your own job title.

RESEARCHERS, DEVELOPERS, INVENTORS

High-tech developments usually move in either of two directions: from a discovery in the laboratory out into the marketplace, or from an unmet need in the marketplace that is communicated to researchers in the laboratory. In either case, the innovation arises from the efforts of teams of people—scientists, business developers, marketers and salespeople, market research analysts. The classic concept of the individual inventor still exists—the U.S. Patent Office reports that about 13 percent of all patents are won by individual inventors—but this indicates their relatively minor part of the innovation process. Moreover, only a small fraction of the individual inventors' developments could be considered high tech.

For most of the twentieth century, a large portion of new technology development came either from corporate research centers or from university or federally funded laboratories. American Telephone and Telegraph (AT&T) had its famous Bell Labs; IBM had the Thomas Watson Research Center; DuPont had Experimental Station No. 1; Xerox had its Palo Alto Research Center; and there were numerous others. Innovations ranging from satellite communications to the personal computer originated as research topics in these centers, which existed primarily among the largest corporations and represented those companies' efforts to foster pure research. The scientists and technologists who worked there had only very general goals to pursue—researching new types of materials, finding out what the latest analytical instruments could do, or trying to understand the basic forces of nature. These large corporations had numerous other laboratories or development centers where commercial or product-oriented research was conducted.

Two things happened toward the end of the twentieth century that changed the nature of these centers. First, several laws were passed by the U.S. government that made it easier for universities to obtain patents to innovations emerged from the laboratories of their faculties and therefore own the commercial rights to these innovations. Second, most corporations became much more focused on commercial development; so-called blue-sky research became less prominent. Today, many corporations still support basic research, but usually as a smaller part of an overall effort to develop commercially viable technologies. A third possible reason for the change was simply that basic research, in many cases (but certainly not all), has become very expensive.

One notable exception to the diminution of private industry–funded basic research is pharmaceutical and biotech research, much of which is still conducted at corporate laboratories. Here there is a complex interplay among corporate laboratories, universities, and federal agencies such as the National Institutes of Health that fund basic medical or biological research. Another key component is the existence of funding from investors, usually known as venture capital investors, who are willing to bet that scientists' research could pay off financially in the development of a new drug, analytical technique, or other innovation.

During World War II, the federal government dedicated enormous resources to developing new weapons to help win the war, most notably the Manhattan Project that led to the development of the atomic bomb. After the war, reflecting on their success, government leaders recognized that there were many aspects of science and technology that should be continued, not only to develop military technology, but also in support of new industries. There was a drive to convert the knowledge of nuclear weapons to nuclear power, to advance the technology of rockets and space travel, and to improve the relatively primitive computers that had been developed during the war. This realization led to the development of a network of federally funded laboratories, many of which are now well-known research centers, such as Los Alamos, Argonne, Lawrence Berkeley, and Brookhaven. Work continues apace at these centers; the federal government supports about 40 percent of the nation's R&D, either through these centers or through direct funding of universities or private industry.

This leads to the third significant part of the R&D scene: university research centers. Years ago, there were mostly informal arrangements between research faculty at a university and local private industry. Now and then a business manager would hire local university faculty to help in some development. This has become much more formalized today, with industrial liaison offices at universities that negotiate arrangements with private industry and with the federal government through the National Science Foundation, the National Institutes of Health, the Department of Defense, and other agencies willing to support university-based research.

In the past ten to twenty years, these industry-university-government collaborations have jumped to yet another level of complexity; now, where industry chooses to locate new facilities often depends on the availability of good schools, with both top-notch faculty and a steady stream of well-trained graduates that are available for employment. This is the Silicon Valley model that was discussed in Chapter 2.

For all of these conditions of geography, tradition, and relationships, the best way to approach thinking about high-tech careers is to start by looking at how science and engineering education is organized on university campuses. Then we'll look at the types of jobs that exist within those academic disciplines.

THE NATURAL AND SOCIAL SCIENCES

High-tech work, naturally enough, is dominated by the scientific and engineering professions. Among scientists, a distinction is usually made between the hard or natural sciences and the soft or social sciences. Examples of the former include geology, physics, biology, and chemistry; examples of the latter include psychology, sociology, and anthropology.

The hard sciences aren't so named because they are difficult to learn (although learning them is not easy), but because they encompass subjects for which experiments can be conducted and results obtained that represent universal scientific truth. For example, a chemist can measure the atomic weight of an element, and that weight will be true for that element anywhere on earth. The scientific knowledge has been reduced to "hard" numerical data.

In the social, or soft, sciences experiments are conducted, but their results tend to be specific to one time and one place. A sociologist might measure the number of high school dropouts in a city school system and attempt to account for the reasons teenagers do not finish school. That numerical data may change from year to year, however, and it certainly changes from one country to another. It is a "soft" result.

NATURAL SCIENCE AND ENGINEERING DISCIPLINES

Here is a list of the major natural sciences, based on the tabulation the U.S. Department of Education uses when accounting for college graduates. (Academic departments in Canada are set up much the same way, although the overall number of graduates each year is far fewer than the number of U.S. grads.)

Agricultural sciences (animal and food sciences, soil science, and
   related fields)
Biology
   Biochemistry
   Botany
   Cell and molecular biology
   Ecology, marine biology, and other specialties
   Microbiology
   Zoology

Computer and information sciences
Health sciences
   Nursing
   Pharmacy
   Predentistry
   Premedicine
   Preveterinary
   Public health
Mathematics
   Pure and applied mathematics
   Statistics
Physical sciences
   Astronomy and astrophysics
   Atmospheric science
   Chemistry
   Earth science
   Geological sciences
   Physics

Another major grouping is the engineering disciplines. The U.S. Department of Education lists twenty-eight distinct engineering specialties, but the main groups are the following fifteen:

Aerospace engineering
Agricultural engineering
Bioengineering
Chemical engineering
Civil, environmental, and architectural engineering
Computer engineering
Electrical and electronics engineering
Engineering physics and mechanics
Geological engineering
Industrial engineering
Materials and metallurgical engineering
Mechanical engineering
Nuclear engineering
Petroleum engineering
Systems engineering

The third major grouping is that of science and engineering technologies. Most of these disciplines parallel the same academic departments in the natural sciences or engineering, but the curriculum is quite different. The key groupings are as follows:

Architectural and civil engineering technology
Electrical and electronics engineering technology
Industrial production and manufacturing engineering technology
Mechanical engineering technology

Not all scientists, engineers, and technologists work in high-tech industries, and there are quite a few high-tech workers who did not study these disciplines while in college. Nevertheless, these programs represent the core of the high-tech workforce. High-tech workers who are actively researching and developing the new technologies of tomorrow will either have college training in these disciplines or will have work training or experience that compensates for the lack of college training.

JOB TITLES ON CAMPUS

Everyone can recognize what the key occupation is at a university: the professor. Being a college professor is a logical goal for some high-tech workers, but that job title also represents the "winners" in a years-long career path. There are many intermediate steps leading up to full professorship.

In the next section of this book, we'll look at factors to consider when deciding whether to get an advanced degree (a master's or doctorate) as part of a decision to be a high-tech worker. However, to be a university professor, there is practically no decision to make; you have to obtain a master's degree and then a doctorate merely to be in the running for a professorship. (There are some academic paths that go from the bachelor's degree directly into the doctoral program, but if the goal is a professorship the difference is minor.)

Having obtained a bachelor's degree, an aspiring professor then enters a master's degree program, which is usually characterized by two to four years of academic study. Qualifications for obtaining a master's degree, such as the number of academic credits required, vary among schools and professions. Master's degree students frequently work part-time as teaching assistants or laboratory assistants at universities while completing their studies.

After the master's degree, the aspiring professor enters a doctoral program. The scope and complexity of these programs vary widely, but usually include additional course work. In addition, the doctoral candidate takes on a formal research project under the guidance of a professor. The professor might have his or her own research program, and the doctoral student might work on projects associated with that program. The research project usually is connected to the dissertation—a summary of the doctoral student's research that is reviewed by the faculty as a requirement for the degree. There are numerous instances of a dissertation leading to the development of a commercial technology. There are also numerous examples of graduate students being engaged in a variety of research topics, perhaps in the process of choosing one for a dissertation or perhaps simply out of curiosity in exploring technology. Sergey Brin and Larry Page, cofounders of Google, were both in the doctoral program in computer science at Stanford University when they founded their pioneering company. Some doctoral students never quite get to finishing their dissertation (leading to the facetiously designated status of ABD, or "all but dissertation"). These students probably already have qualified for a master's degree; they might also be well qualified for an industry research position, but they will probably not qualify for a faculty position.

After completing their dissertation, many Ph.D. graduates aim for an academic posting. The usual entry-level position is as an assistant professor. Many schools—especially the top-ranked ones—hire assistant professors for tenure-track or non-tenure-track positions. A tenure track means that the assistant professor is intended eventually to be evaluated by the faculty for a tenured position, which guarantees continued employment at that institution for the rest of his or her career. Having tenure gives the professor the freedom to explore widely in new areas of science without the pressure of producing immediate results. Assistant professors eventually become associate or full professors; some then take on management responsibilities at the school as deans or department heads.

Ph.D. graduates can also take advantage of short-term work positions on university campuses known as post-doc (post-doctoral) assignments. These jobs usually run for a year or two, and they represent a chance for the Ph.D. graduate to learn how another research center operates or to explore ongoing research interests. The jobs are not meant to be long-term employment (although there is no rule against that); they're more of a way for the Ph.D. graduate to gain more experience while seeking a faculty posting and for research programs being run by faculty professors to gain the expertise of a well-trained Ph.D.

Because some universities have laboratory facilities with hundreds of employees and dozens of labs, technical centers, and related resources, they are themselves employers of engineers, nonfaculty scientists, and other high-tech workers. One of the strengths of a large research university is that there are so many opportunities for research and work for graduate students, even undergraduates, that correlate very well with research jobs in private industry.

JOB TITLES AT GOVERNMENT OR PRIVATE LABORATORIES

As previously mentioned, the federal government devotes billions of dollars to funding scientific research. A significant chunk of this goes out from the National Science Foundation (NSF) and the National Institutes of Health (NIH) to academia; there is rigorous competition among academics to obtain this funding, and many academic research programs would shut down if the federal dollars were cut off. But the federal government also has its own, quite large, network of laboratories. In many cases, these laboratories perform work that is necessary primarily or exclusively for government purposes: developing weapons for the military, for example. In other cases, government and private industry share a stake in developing a technology, such as for aircraft, energy, or medicine; here the pattern is for some research to be carried out in the national laboratory and some to be carried out by private industry, often with government funding. A third category of government research is in conjunction with regulatory activities. The National Institute of Standards and Technology (NIST), for example, is the oldest federal laboratory; it was founded in 1901 as the National Bureau of Standards, with the goal of defining weights, measures, and other numerical descriptions of physical quantities so that everyone could use the same definitions. Another example is the Environmental Protection Agency (EPA), which conducts field research to monitor the quality of air, water, and ecosystems to support regulatory activity. The EPA also funds academic and industrial research.

Job titles at the national laboratories are fairly straightforward: technician, scientist, engineer, and so on, with various numerical rankings within each job class. An important managerial role is the program manager, who might either manage a team of researchers within a laboratory or oversee and evaluate the quality of work being performed by a private industry contractor under a federal grant. Many of the research jobs require a doctoral degree, the same as a university-based research position, but there are also jobs for bachelor's or master's degree holders.

JOB TITLES IN PRIVATE INDUSTRY

It is usually the case that there are several, or even hundreds, of companies competing in the marketplace to win business from customers. Some of these companies are very successful; some are only moderately so, and some drop out after a few years. From this situation, it is easy to reason that different companies are organized differently, or have a variety of work processes, and put an emphasis on different aspects of the business. And from that, it is straightforward to conclude that job titles vary not only from industry to industry, but also from company to company within an industry.

Job titles have become quite theatrical among some companies in recent years. Numerous high-tech companies, especially in the software arena, have a "chief evangelist," who speaks at industry events to try to promote a company's technology. Top researchers are "visionaries;" customer service representatives have become "customer experience managers."

But before you can get to such unusual job positions, there are a several groups of more conventional job titles to consider. Modern high-tech companies tend to be organized as teams dedicated to specific functions.

- **Researcher, scientist.** The people who work in the laboratories on advanced areas of science that may or may not have a commercial application.
- **Development engineer, applications engineer, applications scientist.** The experts at developing a technology so that it has commercial applications.
- **Design engineer, test engineer, systems engineer.** The group of specialists who might, for example, develop the next version of a product. Systems work implies that a variety of technical subsystems need to be brought together as a unified whole. An

automobile, to take one simple example, needs specialists in materials, engines, controls, structures, and other specialties. Systems engineers pay attention to how all the components come together.

There is a parallel structure for software and communication networks: researchers or computer scientists, software developers, systems or network engineers and administrators, and then programmers and testing engineers.

Both for high-tech systems and software, at some point in the development process experts in user interfaces, human factors engineering, or some type of industrial design need to be brought into the process. For example, a modern aircraft's cockpit needs to be analyzed for how well pilots can understand and react to the huge array of sensors, controls, and warning lights on the control panel. Internet websites call for usability experts who can predict how the typical site visitor will make use of their features. Even a product that is never touched by the individual customer—say, a hydraulic subsystem on a rocket—needs to be analyzed for how it will be serviced by maintenance engineers or technicians. The human element never entirely disappears from even the highest of high tech.

From research to user interface, these tasks are centered around inventing or developing a new product. Once the design is finalized, the product must be manufactured in quantity. There are numerous high-tech products that are one-of-a-kind—the NASA Space Shuttle program, for example, or the prototype of a new scientific instrument—but many high-tech products are intended to be high-volume consumer products. High-tech manufacturing is not too different from other types of manufacturing, with the possible exception that the manufacturing team must usually deal with rapidly changing or evolving technical specifications. We see this phenomenon in consumer electronics all the time: the new version of a personal computer, television, or telephone is almost always just around the corner. The price of many high-tech products drops steadily over the life of each version. In software development, customers are now accustomed to new revisions to existing software packages appearing a few times annually. Design specifications never quite settle down into one version that gets manufactured for years.

Manufacturing is its own body of knowledge; it is possible to study the topic of manufacturing engineering itself at many schools. The job titles involved with manufacturing are, typically, production engineer, plant engineer, operations manager, and quality engineer or specialist. These types of titles are common in all types of manufacturing. The high-tech field of software design, however, doesn't really have a manufacturing step (except for the relatively trivial process of making copies of a program, packaging those copies, and shipping them out); rather, once the software developers and programmers are done writing code, the product is essentially finished. There are, however, specialized activities involved with quality control and what is called validation, meaning that the code must be tested in a variety of real-world applications to ensure that it is bug-free.

While we're on the topic of manufacturing, it is worth noting that there are high-tech applications in what otherwise might be considered conventional manufacturing processes. The use of robots on a production line that is making, say, plumbing parts is an example. In fact, across the entire range of manufacturing processes, there has been a general trend of developing automated systems and computer controls to meet more precise specifications, ensure more consistent quality, and lower production costs. These job functions will be touched on in later chapters on mechanical engineering, robotics, and automation.

The next, and basically last, step in high-tech businesses is installing the device, product, or software system at the client's site, or delivering it to stores where it is sold. Many high-tech products need very sophisticated procedures for installation and setup. They might also need regular servicing. Jobs with these responsibilities have titles like field service engineer, service technician, maintenance engineer, or application specialist. Software companies spend considerable effort on the installation of their systems, especially if they are large software systems that handle multiple functions for the customer. Installation and service are critical functions for many companies because the service engineer or technician is the person in most constant contact with the customer. Companies know that they depend on repeat business from existing customers, and they will invest in training their field service workers to provide high-quality service and at the same time "hold the hand" of the customer.

NONTECH WORKERS IN HIGH TECH

At this point it is important to note that only part of the high-tech workforce is comprised of professionals engaged in research and development.

The annals of business history are filled with failed companies that had large staffs of top engineers and scientists, yet still went out of business because they were unable to commercialize or market a new technology. Today, additional types of professional experts are needed, especially in small, new firms trying to bring a new technology to the market.

These experts include lawyers (especially those experienced in patent law), sales and marketing professionals, communications experts (especially technical writers), business administrators, and human resources managers. Usually high-tech industries hire people with liberal arts backgrounds for these types of jobs. A college graduate with a degree in, say, English or history will be challenged to learn about the technology that his or her employer is developing. The best graduates will be able to cope with this challenge. Having a technical undergraduate degree is certainly not a drawback for taking a nontechnical job in this environment, and it can often be an asset. But in this case, the job candidate must meet the opposite challenge: proving that his or her marketing, communications, or administrative skills are strong.

CHAPTER

4

EDUCATION AND CAREER PLANNING

EXPLORING HIGH-TECH CAREERS

What should you do to get the information to make the best career choices? Without question, the hands-down action to take is to jump onto the Internet. The Internet is an exceptionally good source of information about all sorts of professions and hobbies, but it is clearly biased toward the very people that invented it—the high-tech workforce. The Internet also eliminates the traditional problem people living away from large urban areas have contended with—the lack of information resources close by. Many schools provide Internet access for their students, and some forward-thinking communities make it available as a resource for residents.

The wealth of information available on the Internet is, however, also one of its problems. It is hard to sift through all the data and all the conversations, to find the most useful information. A good first step might be to go to the websites of professional societies described in this book (see the Appendix). Most of them are open to the public, and some have special sections for students. Usually the national or international headquarters of these professional societies have the largest reservoir of information, including contact information.

A second step is to follow your contact at the national level with contact at the local level. If you live near practically any major urban area—and quite a few suburban or rural areas as well—these professional societies will have local chapters that are accessible to you. Get in touch with the local leaders of these organizations and ask if you can attend the regular meetings, which are sometimes held monthly. Periodically, too, the local chapter will host a national meeting, which will bring professionals from around the country to your region. For the best organizations, the national meeting is usually an occasion for papers to be presented by experts in their field. These presentations are often very informative. Try to get permission to sit in on them.

In a similar vein, nearly every professional organization of any significant size has an in-house journal or magazine that informs its members of significant happenings within the profession. Usually these journals are obtained through membership in the organization, which would keep most high school students out of the picture.

Again, if you live in a major urban area, you can gain access to these journals by going to nearly any large urban library. If there is a college or university in your area, you will also find most of these journals at the school's library. (You will almost never find these publications for sale at a newsstand, but that doesn't mean that they aren't worth reading.) Read the journals closely, especially those that report news of the profession as well as publish research papers. Look at the advertisements in them and try to figure out what value that equipment or service has to a profession.

It is worthwhile to read these journals or to attend society meetings not only to gain useful technical knowledge that you can apply while you go on to college, but also to gain a sense of the people and issues within that profession. Leave yourself open to the *feel* of the information you are getting, rather than the factual content. Would you be happy with these people as your coworkers? Are the subjects that concern them something you are curious about?

There are also many other avenues for obtaining information about a high-tech profession, often through your high school science teachers or guidance counselors. Make use of them, too.

The value of all these forms of contact is to give you insight into what the future holds and to provide role models of people whose work or attitudes toward their careers will help motivate you. Studying science or engineering at nearly any college is a difficult undertaking, and the programs are often too concentrated on technical learning and not concentrated enough on what to do with that technical learning. This is an unfortunate, but probably necessary, obstacle to a high-tech career. Most science and engineering students are of little value to a researcher or employer until the basic technical knowledge is obtained.

COLLEGE—MAYBE?

Most of this chapter—indeed, most of this book—is premised on getting a college degree as the first step toward a high-tech career. Sharp students of the recent history of high tech, though, will be able to cite a number of examples of successful high-tech workers who do not have a college degree. Perhaps the most notable example is Bill Gates, chairman of Microsoft Corporation, who had matriculated to Harvard University in the early 1970s, but left when he and some friends started doing some programming for what were the earliest forms of personal computers. Roughly a decade later, Michael Dell, founder of Dell, Inc., one of the largest personal computer suppliers in the world, did the same thing, leaving the University of Texas at Austin after his freshman year to start his business.

High tech is sometimes like that. The right combination of technology development, business opportunity, and innate skills come together, and a career can get started. This circumstance seems to have been especially true in the early days of the personal computer, and then again in the early days of the Internet during the 1990s. It takes a strong ego to be an inventor or to start one's own business; going to college doesn't necessarily strengthen one's ego or enhance the quality of a bright idea one might have that could be the start of a new business. There is also the matter of being in the right place at the right time; some technological innovations are just waiting to burst out as new products or businesses, and if you're perceptive enough to recognize those opportunities, you might also recognize that the competition is not going to wait for you to finish college or add another diploma to your wall.

But—and this is a very big qualifier—most areas of high tech require a deep understanding not just of science or engineering, but also of what works in the business world. The landscape of the technological world is littered with the wreckage of exciting new inventions that never became commercial. Having a bright idea is not the only prerequisite for a career in high tech; it must be the first of many more bright ideas that need to be thought out along the way to a successful business or invention. There are quite a few situations where one can test out a new idea at low cost and, if it doesn't work, change it or move on to another bright idea. But the majority of high-tech applications require an expensive investment in researchers, laboratories, and business managers. High-tech companies may always worry about whether their organizations are properly set up to develop new products and businesses, but they rarely question the billions of dollars they invest in R&D, because experience has taught them that investment has to be made to begin the process.

A similar thought process can go on regarding yourself. If you have confidence in your abilities, you will want to invest in those abilities with the kind of training that a college degree provides. The body of knowledge that constitutes science and technology is vast, and it is growing larger every day. Learning how to deal with this body of knowledge is one of the key objectives of a college degree.

Another argument can be made simply on the basis of numbers. For every Bill Gates or Michael Dell, there are tens of thousands of scientists, business managers, and technologists who have obtained two, three, or even more degrees. The overall national statistics show that over the course of a career, having a college degree results in a 25 percent or more increase in income. And while we enjoy the romantic notion of the lone entrepreneur or lone inventor whose ideas become successful, the reality is that most people work as employees of organizations, and most organizations want to hear about your college degree from the moment they meet you. For many organizations, the lack of a college degree means that the door to the employment office will never open.

The flip side of the college experience is also worth considering—that college will be the source of the ideas that lead to a high-tech career. A few students go to college with a very specific goal in mind and charge forward in pursuit of that goal. But most go to college to learn more about the world around them as part of the process of choosing a career. Even if a student has a very clear vision of a future as a scientist or engineer, college will provide the map to find which type of science or engineering is best pursued. Finally, most colleges, especially those with a strong research component, are hotbeds of new ideas, bright people, and visionary teachers. It's not an accident that some people have hatched a new business or started on the path to an invention while at college. They formed those ideas because they were at a place where innovation is encouraged.

MAJOR CHOICES

Time after time, guidance counselors and career advisers, when asked by a student, "What should I study, and what career should I follow?" tell the student, "Do what you are good at and enjoy doing and what meets your needs for financial security." At the beginning of most people's careers, financial needs are not as great as they are later in life, so really the issue boils down to finding a field of education and work that interests you.

Frequently, however, too many students make decisions for a college major and a career on the basis of what is hot or in demand at the time they enter college. This is a serious mistake for several reasons.

First, it is often the case that what was a hot field when you entered college has cooled noticeably by the time you graduate. (Don't be alarmed if this is what happens; there are things you can do to make the best of the situation.)

Second, you may be denying your true abilities if you study a subject only because of its assumed job potential after you graduate. Our daily work occupies at least half of our waking existence; why spend this time doing something you do not enjoy? Moreover, the best work is usually performed by people who enjoy what they are doing. Do yourself, those around you, and your future employer a favor and choose a major that fulfills your personal interests.

Third, it is becoming more and more uncommon for someone to study a professional topic in college, join a company to practice that profession, and spend the next forty years working at that job for one employer. More and more, people switch jobs, voluntarily or involuntarily, during their careers. Numerous surveys show that a worker who has had three or four employers by the time he or she is middle-aged earns more and has a higher position than one who does not move about. If you study a field that doesn't appeal to you to begin with, your ability to grow in that field or to use your job experience as a springboard to another line of work is limited.

Fourth, college is easy for many people, but it is not easy for many students who choose majors in science or engineering disciplines. The work is demanding, and the competition is often intense. It doesn't make sense to put yourself through a major that you have no personal attachment to.

College is a time to experiment, to find yourself in the various subjects and disciplines that you are exposed to. This experimenting works best when you give each subject your best shot. If you are majoring in something that is of no interest to you, you have limited your opportunities to experiment.

Another factor to consider is how closely a particular college major is matched to the work performed in specific high-tech industries.

Some majors are closely tied to professional work: microelectronic chip design, for example, is performed primarily by electronics engineers. But who is involved in the development of nanomaterials? Physicists and chemists analyze molecular structures. Chemical engineers and materials scientists work out production methods. Mechanical engineers, chemists, biomedical engineers, and others develop applications. Numerous studies of technology development have shown that the work is becoming increasingly cross-disciplinary; many different types of expertise are involved. To some degree, the major you choose can be influenced by the resources and programs at the college you choose. In other cases, you will attempt to turn yourself into a cross-disciplinary team of one by choosing a combination of a major and a minor concentration.

Having said all this, it may still be very difficult to select a major that you will enjoy. It is easy after college is done to look back at good and bad choices. It is very difficult to do this while looking ahead. This is where some familiarity with people who practice in a field that is of interest to you comes in. Ask them what they majored in and why. Ask them what was good and bad about their education and how valuable it is to their work today. Take advantage of the experiences of others.

COLLEGE PREPARATION

Alternatively, some students, and some employers, seek to cross the gap between the technical and the nontechnical aspects of a career by matching an undergraduate degree in some technical field with another degree. Some students carry a double major, such as business and engineering. This has the advantage of reducing the cost of higher education for the student by keeping the time necessary to gain both degrees to four or five years. It is, of course, a heavy load to carry during one's college years.

More commonly, students major in one program as an undergraduate and then study another discipline in graduate school. Some typical combinations are an undergraduate degree in engineering or science and a graduate degree in business. Technologist/lawyer is another combination. Some students go on to graduate school immediately after earning an undergraduate degree; others work for a few years in their chosen field before returning to the college campus. Yet others enter graduate programs in night school while holding down a daytime job.

A third course of action is to seek a cross-disciplinary major that offers exactly the combination one seeks. A close review of college catalogs reveals programs with names like Technology and Public Policy (great training for a career in a government research agency), Technology Management, Information Systems Management, Communications Management (the combination of training in telecommunications and business management), and many others. The great majority of colleges in both the United States and Canada allow students to devise their own program of study, as independent majors, as long as certain academic standards are met. Generally speaking, these independent major programs work best for the students who know exactly what they want to do during their career. One drawback of such a tailored college education is that unless an employer is seeking just that combination of interests when the student graduates, a job may be hard to find.

One of the more exciting career endeavors these days, and one that is often best addressed by a cross-disciplinary degree, is environmental work. It is possible to study environmental engineering or natural resources programs such as forestry to gain a foothold in the percolating environmental field. But the cross-disciplinary programs enable students to get a broader understanding of the environmental issues of the day and to make themselves more acceptable as job candidates to a wider range of employers.

As these options indicate, the challenge in preparing for a high-tech career is not in finding the right program to study—there are many options and many strategies that the student can adopt. The real challenge is in making decisions about where one's interests lie. Keep in mind that the choices are yours.

BACHELOR'S, MASTER'S, OR DOCTORATE?

In a great many professions a bachelor's degree is sufficient. A student may choose to go on to graduate school, but except in selected areas like medicine or teaching, an advanced degree simply makes one somewhat more employable or possibly worth a higher salary. (In medicine and teaching there are many career positions that simply are not accessible to the bachelor's graduate.)

In most of the sciences there are two distinct tracks that graduates can follow based on their degree level. In most cases, R&D positions are open to those with advanced degrees but relatively limited for those with only a bachelor's degree. If you want to work in the laboratory of a major corporation, top university, or prestigious private research organization, make preparations for continuing your schooling. You might need to alter your undergraduate course load somewhat to take courses that will be a useful preparation for graduate school—acquiring expertise in a foreign language is one example.

This certainly doesn't mean that only a Ph.D. scientist can be a high-tech worker. The work in commercializing new scientific knowledge in the form of useful products requires extensive work in process design, manufacturing methods, marketing, and technical service. All these job positions are usually available to the bachelor's graduate.

While it is possible to obtain a master's degree in most of the sciences, there are not many job positions specifically geared to the master's-level graduate. Having this degree certainly makes the graduate more employable relative to those with only a bachelor's degree, but very often the master's graduate winds up competing against bachelor's degree holders for the same jobs. Most teaching positions at universities require the doctorate; most R&D positions in laboratories call for that degree as well.

In the engineering disciplines there are five distinct educational goals that can be sought. One is the bachelor's degree alone, which is the training that most engineers stop with. It is a testament to the value of an engineering degree that very often this is all the college-level education an engineer needs for a lifelong career. To be sure, a good engineer will continue to learn as his or her career progresses by attending technical meetings, signing up for seminars sponsored by an employer, or gaining admission to company training programs. Many of the professional societies listed in the Appendix sponsor continuing education programs to further enhance engineers' skills.

Many baccalaureate engineers go on to obtain a master's in business administration (M.B.A.) with the expectation that the two degrees will help them rise into management positions in technology-driven companies. Some engineers feel that the conventional M.B.A. degree, which usually involves the study of finance, economics, and related topics, is not closely enough connected to technology management. For this reason some schools have started programs in management of technology or manufacturing technology as a better alternative to the conventional M.B.A.

Another choice is to pursue a professional engineer's (PE) license. This certification is provided by all fifty states and requires passing two tests and gaining several years' experience in working under the guidance of engineers who themselves have PE licenses. With a PE license an engineer has a more prestigious achievement record to present to potential employers and can also do certain types of work (the design of public buildings, for example) that unlicensed engineers are not permitted to do.

There are definitely good reasons for having a PE license; nevertheless, only about a quarter or so of working engineers have bothered to earn it, and most of those are civil engineers. The simple fact of the matter is that in many types of work, a PE license is not a requirement.

The fourth choice is to obtain a master's degree in engineering. Most of the time this degree level demonstrates to an employer that a job candidate has a serious commitment to the technology of his or her major. In certain fields, such as semiconductor design, computer science, factory automation, and others, the technology is moving so fast and the necessary knowledge for professional practice is growing so much that a master's degree is simply a way of keeping up with change. For this reason many engineers get a job after earning their bachelor's degree and then study for a master's at evening school. Often an engineer's employer will cover the cost of this advanced education.

A variation on the master's degree track is to obtain a master's in an engineering or science program other than what one studied as an undergraduate. This doesn't work equally well for all combinations of undergraduate and master's programs. Depending on the choices, the student may wind up needing more undergraduate-level courses to meet the requirements of the master's program or may find that the master's degree in one field has little to do with employment in another. This is definitely a situation where career advice from college deans or from employment professionals is helpful.

The fifth option, of course, is to obtain a doctorate in engineering. This qualifies the engineer to teach and to perform R&D in nearly all technologies. There are Ph.D. engineers who perform basic research developing new techniques for microelectronics design, writing computer software, or designing advanced materials. There are others whose work is geared more toward applications in the commercial world, such as designing better automobiles, more energy-efficient power generators, or more wholesome foods. The choice is up to the individual.

As all these choices indicate, there are many career paths open to the high-tech worker. The educational requirements are demanding, but the rewards are plentiful. Contact the professional and educational organizations listed in the Appendix for more information. Make researching a career as important as the study you put into any of the courses you are taking now or while you are in college.

CAREER DEVELOPMENT WHILE IN COLLEGE

Over one hundred years ago, as the modern style of research university became established in the United States, most students went to college to get a very abstract training in what they were studying. Ph.D.-level scientists or engineers primarily thought of themselves as pure researchers and teachers; their goal was to gain a professorship at some university. In later decades, and especially since the 1970s, many universities have recognized that, while some of their students have academic aspirations, most of them plan on careers in industrial research or business. Many universities have responded to this changed emphasis by aligning the educational curriculum more closely with what private industry is looking for: graduates who can enter into a work assignment, ready to go, the day after they graduate.

The best way to accomplish that readiness, for most curricula, is to include some type of work experience in the college career. There are a variety of approaches, but the goals are similar: to expose students to real-world applications of what they are learning in the classroom and to allow the students to become familiar with the culture of industrial research and development.

The most formal version of this is the cooperative education program, as established at numerous schools around the country, especially in engineering. Students undergo a cycle of two or three semesters on campus, one semester at a job, and then back to campus. (There may or may not be a summer break; it depends on how the cycles are set up.) The program might take five years to complete, but at the end of it, the student has a bachelor's degree plus a year of work experience—often at a paying job whose income can be used to defray college expenses. In some cases, the student is farther along in the process of obtaining a PE license, which requires work experience under the supervision of licensed engineers. Finally, employers are getting a preview of the capabilities of the co-op student, and an employer might be in a position to offer the student a job upon graduation.

A less formal, but still powerful training boost can be obtained from internship programs, usually over the summer recess, and sometimes arranged under the auspices of the university. Many research-oriented universities have numerous laboratory or technical jobs available to students, with eligibility for these jobs possibly based on qualifying for financial aid.

Finally, the thought processes of the business world have seeped into university course work. Numerous universities have set up entrepreneurship programs, where students develop a project as if it were a business proposal to attract funding for commercialization. Some of these programs provide prize money to winners; some result in actual funding. On a less competitive level, schools offer concentrations in business management, technology development, or research to expose students to the realities of the business world.

Co-op programs and internships work well for undergraduate education; at the master's and doctoral levels, the students might have part-time jobs. A common practice for many newly graduated engineers or scientists is to continue study via evening programs for an M.B.A or technical degree. Many employers—especially among the high-tech companies—will fund some or all of the cost of these programs. It's an intensive situation requiring much time and work for a couple of years, but the investment in the advanced training can pay off fairly quickly in promotions or better job opportunities.

PART TWO

The High-Tech Industries

As detailed in Chapter 2, high-tech industries are characterized by advanced scientific or engineering principles, a radically different way of doing things (as opposed to incremental improvement), and dramatic commercial potential if successful. High-tech projects are inherently risky; their chances for ultimate success are very unclear at the outset, and frequently, they evolve along the way, perhaps starting as a small, specialized effort that suddenly becomes a broad-based area of application (the opposite—a large research project "spinning off" many small technological developments— can also occur. NASA's planetary probes, for example, have accelerated development in robotics and communications.)

Talking about early high-tech projects implies that there is a time element to high tech, too. Today's low-tech businesses or applications were yesterday's high-tech ones. Over time, a successful new technology becomes the normal way of doing things—and the sort of thing that the next high-tech application may supplant. As this third edition was going to press, for example, numerous people were marking the twenty-fifth anniversary of the IBM-type personal computer (which wasn't the first PC, but has certainly proven to be the most successful commercially). In 1981, when this product was introduced, it created a sensation and became an entire high-tech world of its own. Today, even though PC components continue to evolve, PC manufacturing is turning into a low-tech commodity business, with vendors competing mostly on price.

Another risk factor that affects the progress of new technologies is how social needs evolve. Today, for example, a host of new governmental and social concerns revolve around national security and the threat of terrorist attacks; a number of technologies, ranging from x-ray scanning of entire truck containers to sophisticated chemical and radiation analyzers, have been developed to improve airline and shipborne security. Sometimes these social needs arise rapidly (in this case, in the aftermath of the 9/11 attacks on New York and Washington, D.C.); in other cases, they are a gradual or predictable process of increasing attention, and companies or individuals who seek to develop a new technology to meet such a need are gambling that the timing is right. The rapid increase in the cost of motor fuel in the past few years is a good example of this; the high attention that energy is garnering today is an echo of a similar situation in the late 1970s.

All of these considerations play into how one goes about choosing a high-tech industry or application area. Government agencies and think tanks used to devote considerable effort to identifying critical technologies for which government resources and funding were to be gathered. In recent years, this type of forecasting has gone out of style; the main thrust of the White House American Competitiveness Initiative, for example, focuses on creating the right environment to foster technology development through educational resources, tax credits, and supporting technologies such as instruments or computational resources and letting private industry decide which technologies to pursue.

Still, we have to start somewhere. Using a compilation of the various lists of high-tech areas described in Chapter 2 and making some rule-of-thumb estimates of how broadly a new technology might be applied (and therefore how many jobs might be generated), here is a list of high technologies that provides an overview of the field as of the early years of this century. The technology areas listed here will be reviewed in the next six chapters.

Key High-Tech Groups
Advanced Materials and Materials Processing
Biotechnology
Medical Technology and Health Care
Electronics, Computers, and Communications
Information Technology
Energy and the Environment

Part of the responsibility of anyone who wants to be a high-tech worker is to keep current with where technology is going. There are numerous resources to consult to do this; these are listed in the Appendix.

C H A P T E R

ADVANCED MATERIALS AND MATERIALS PROCESSING

"The New Alchemy" is the title *Business Week* magazine used to describe the revolution going on in materials technologies. Alchemy, of course, was the search by scientists/magicians in medieval times to find a way to transmute base materials such as earth into gold. While this goal was never achieved, the ancient alchemists did develop many types of knowledge that later scientists were able to put to good use.

In the twentieth century, that age-old goal of transmuting materials became a reality with the dawn of the atomic age. Physicists who run large accelerators—machines that fire atoms against each other at high speeds—are able to combine atomic particles almost at will, turning one element into another. The catch is that this method of making a material such as gold is much, much more expensive than digging it out of the ground.

Nevertheless, once scientists were able to devise tools for changing atoms or for directing them precisely to a specific location, a great variety of new applications opened up. For many such researchers, the model seems to replicate life itself—to be able to very accurately manufacture the molecules that make up seashells, spiderwebs, or tree branches. When you look at a microphotograph of, say, a leaf, the first thing you notice is the startling beauty of how cells interconnect with each other and how they support the leaf's structure. If human researchers are able to replicate such detailed structures in an economical fashion, they have the potential of making better materials for everything from coffee cups to the struts that support the International Space Station.

Today much of the current excitement on materials focuses on nano-materials, defined as designed atomic or molecular structures on the scale of 100 nanometers or less (a human hair is about 75,000 nm). There is more than a little hype to the topic, but very real value is being created.

MATERIALS

What are materials? They are the substances that are refined into some consistent form and content and then shaped into useful articles. The traditional classes of materials are metals, ceramics, and fibers. Human civilization is partially defined by the movement from the Stone Age (stones are a type of ceramic) into a Bronze and Iron Age (both metals). Along the way humans learned to take natural or refined materials and weave them into cloth or fabrics, which made better clothing, housing, and transportation possible (what would an ancient ship be without its cloth sails?).

In the last century, the big innovation was the development of synthetic polymers—plastics. A polymer is simply a long-chained string of atoms; when these strings are intertwined with each other, a durable yet flexible material is created. Some of the first polymers were developed to replace the fibers obtained from cotton or wool. By the 1940s and 1950s scientists had learned how to manipulate polymers to create films (such as sandwich wrap) and solid sheets or blocks. The advantage of many of these polymers is that they can be molded easily and efficiently. To compare, think about all the steps necessary in forming a metal cup (forming the metal into a sheet, bending the sheet, welding it together somehow, and then bolting a handle onto it) versus making a plastic one (melting the plastic resin and injecting it into a mold, from which the finished article pops out in a few seconds).

When engineers and other researchers began to experiment with plastics in other applications, they quickly discovered a severe limitation. As a sheet or block of plastic gets larger, it becomes weaker. It flexes too much and is prone to crack or warp under relatively low stresses. To get around this, researchers combined plastic resins with glass fibers to form a material we now commonly call fiberglass.

Fiberglass is valuable for applications where the weight of a structure is as important as its strength. These applications include aerospace vehicles, where fiberglass can be used for wings or body fuselages, and boat hulls. Fiberglass is a composite material, meaning simply that it is a combination of two or more different materials. As such, it can be considered to be one of the first modern high-tech materials. Now fiberglass is commonly used in automobiles or for housings for computers or other appliances. It is becoming a more common component of housing construction as well.

In recent years the concept of a composite that combines the advantages of several different materials has become valuable in metals and ceramics. Countertops in kitchens are often a composite of plastic and clay or stone dust—a polymer/ceramic composite. Metals are being sintered (melted together) with ceramic powders—a metal/ceramic composite. Alternatively, a small amount of polymer is often added to concrete mixtures to strengthen them and make them resistant to chipping, a composite that is known as polycrete. Most recently, metallurgists have begun experimenting with mixing one type of metal with another (usually by mixing the two metal powders together and then firing the combination while it is being molded into the desired shape)—a metal matrix.

Some of these composite mixtures have the additional benefit that they can be easily molded—almost as easily as the original plastics were. This is called net shape forming, and it can greatly reduce the cost of machining, say, a toothed gear.

NANOMATERIALS

Nanotechnology is an object lesson in how the path from basic research to commercial products is supposed to work. In the microelectronics industry, new instrumentation and production capabilities over the past few decades have given scientists the ability to examine objects microscopically at the atomic level. On a parallel track, a research chemist at Rice University, Richard Smalley, was investigating the properties of microscopic carbon particles, such as are produced in a smoky flame. Put the two together, and a new molecular form of carbon that its creators called buckminsterfullerene was discovered by Smalley and coworkers in 1986 (they won the Nobel Prize for this discovery a decade later). Initially a mere laboratory curiosity, the material soon became intensively studied because of the structural and chemical properties it exhibited. The analytical and processing techniques soon led to other material discoveries—carbon nanotubes, sheets, and whiskers—and pushed materials scientists to examine other conventional materials, such as gold and other metals, in nano form.

Buckminsterfullerene captured broad public interest because it was a new material (and having such a catchy name probably didn't hurt). A scientist named Eric Drexler put the development of the fullerene family of materials together with other developments in ceramics, metallurgy, and microelectronics as a unified research theme that he called nanotechnology. (A Japanese researcher also used this terminology.) Now nano-level research is going on across a broad range of applications. Nanoparticles of metals have been found to act like liquids and to have different chemical properties from the bulk form of the metal. Nanotubes of various compositions can direct electrons in ways that are different from copper wires or other structures. Nanofilters can separate two materials almost atom by atom. At the far fringes of current research, nanomachines or nanorobots, consisting of mechanical parts built on the molecular scale, are being conceptualized as medical devices, environmental cleanup techniques, or new manufacturing systems.

In the commercial arena, the most success has been seen in carbon or ceramic whiskers, or short fibers, that are being added to plastic, ceramic, and metal composite materials; they provide significant strengthening and resistance to cracking. Nanoscale materials have significant advantages in newer types of batteries, which may ultimately increase the viability of electric vehicles for transportation. A few dozen small startup companies are devoted to commercializing nanotechnology; meanwhile corporate giants like IBM, Toshiba, and others have made multimillion-dollar bets on nanotech research.

At present, nanotechnology is mostly in the hands of Ph.D.-level researchers in chemistry, materials science, physics, or electronic engineering. As the possibility of commercial products opens up, companies will be hiring chemical or manufacturing engineers and others to devise production methods.

ADVANCED MATERIALS

Advanced materials can be thought of in two ways: the chemical makeup of the material itself, or the methods by which it is formed into a commercially useful structure. The realm of materials processing includes a variety of highly specialized structures and compositions. In chemical manufacturing these include catalysts, which are simply substances that speed up a chemical reaction, much as a jolt of adrenaline helps us run faster or harder. Catalysts are often a synthetic analog of a naturally occurring mineral, so catalyst research combines elements of geology and chemistry.

By contrast, there are advanced materials known as membranes, which can be formed from plastics, ceramics, or metals. Membranes are fabricated in such a way that they have microscopically small pores in them. The pores are small enough to exclude some molecules, while allowing others to pass through unimpeded.

The most common use of membranes is to desalinate seawater, making it drinkable. Vast networks of such membranes are now being used in the Middle East, where fresh water is scarce; they are also being considered for use in the drought-stricken regions of California. In industry, membranes are often used to separate air, splitting it into a stream of nearly pure nitrogen and another stream rich in oxygen. Previously nitrogen was available only by chilling air to well below zero so that it liquefied; the nitrogen would freeze before the oxygen did, thus enabling a processor to separate the two. That process is still used, but it is highly energy intensive and is economical only when large amounts are needed. With the new membrane-based systems, volumes of air small enough to run a food-processing shop (where the gas keeps food fresh) or for small-scale metal processing (to keep the metal from rusting or oxidizing while it is being processed) are now feasible.

Mention of below-zero temperatures brings to mind the famed warm superconductors—materials that can conduct electricity with no loss of energy. The property of superconductivity has been known since the beginning of the twentieth century, but has been achieved only with exotic metals cooled to near absolute zero. The new superconductors are basically ceramics—mixtures of copper oxides with other minerals—sintered according to a highly specific formula. Instead of being chilled to near absolute zero, these new mixtures only need to be cooled to about $-280°F$, which is within the range of liquid nitrogen. When warm superconductors were initially developed, it was almost as if Superman's kryptonite had been found: people expected to have impossibly cheap energy and to ride monorails to the moon overnight. Reality soon set in, and scientists are still carefully slogging through a thicket of knotty technical issues relating to the manufacture of large amounts of superconducting material. Good things are in store for warm superconductors, however, especially for microelectronic devices, and the rest may come in time.

A broad area of current and future materials science lies in composites, which are mixtures of different materials in a specified manner. Fiberglass, which has been around for more than fifty years, is one example, although the material (usually a combination of glass fibers in a plastic resin) continually gets new attention. The latest military and commercial aircraft are being fabricated from carbon-fiber matrices to push the capabilities of the composites to the maximum of strength and light weight. The same materials are showing up in high-end golf clubs and bicycle frames.

MATERIALS PROCESSING

It's fun to think about something like the same composite in a military jet wing being used in a bicycle frame, but typically, such applications are only practical when the cost of making the composite can be kept at a reasonable level. This highlights the other component of working with high-tech materials: figuring out how to make them cost-effectively.

A cliché of the engineering world goes like this: "Engineering is figuring out how to do something for a dollar that any darn fool could do for two." The innovation is in figuring out how to lower the production cost of an obviously superior material so that it is cost-competitive with other materials.

Manufacturing methods can garner as many patents as creating new materials, but it is very rare that innovation in this area wins public attention. Today, for example, one of the main holdups to broader commercial application of nanomaterials is the difficulty of producing them in large volumes with consistent quality. Numerous engineers and scientists are addressing the problem by studying more closely the reaction conditions under which they are created and then figuring out how to separate them from unreacted material or waste by-products.

Two dominant themes characterize the current state of the art in advanced manufacturing technology. One is the trend of taking start-and-stop, discontinuous processes and making them continuous. The other is broader use of automation.

Rapid Prototyping

Another term for start-and-stop production is batch production. In steel production, for example, the tradition had been to make hot steel in a blast furnace, then pour the liquid metal into molds, cool it so that it solidified but was still soft, then transfer it to a rolling mill or forge where it could be pressed into a long sheet, rod, or bar. The process was slow, labor-intensive, and wasted much of the energy used to heat the metal. Now, in the process of continuous casting, the liquid metal is poured into a device that allows it to be formed and cooled at the same time. Liquid metal goes in one end; sheets or bars of steel come out the other end. Alternatively, the steps necessary to machine a piece of metal can be simplified if the liquid metal can be cast in a form that is close to the final shape—say, a toothed gear—thus reducing the amount of metal that has to be cut away. The process is known as near net-shape forming.

Both of these innovations are now a few decades old, although there is still ongoing improvement. A radically new type of fabrication called rapid prototyping or digital prototyping holds the promise of revolutionizing many conventional manufacturing techniques. Rapid prototyping starts with the same design software that is used to draw blueprints for shaped products. But instead of transferring those digital drawings to a cutting or shaping machine, which will gradually form the shape out of metal, plastic, or other material, the digital drawings are loaded into a machine that uses a combination of light and special liquid plastics that solidify when exposed to light. In a short time, the virtual shape that existed only in a computer drawing becomes an actual physical shape, which can be used as a prototype for designing the shape in other materials or as the shape around which a mold can be formed. The computer-aided design (CAD) drawings can also be used with other programs to analyze performance characteristics, size limitations, and other manufacturability criteria.

Rapid prototyping is gradually moving into the design of mechanical parts, automotive design, and many consumer goods. The direction of the technology is clear: at some point, it will become possible to start with a computer drawing and end with the actual product at the other end, using a design/fabrication system that might fit on a desktop.

Automation

The second dominant theme of high-tech manufacturing is the use of automation technology. Rapid prototyping combines both digital automation and the batch-to-continuous trend. In many other industries, there have been—and may always be—hundreds or thousands of individual production steps. The use of computers, robots, and information technology, however, are reforming these complex processes. Robots, for example, are sometimes a drop-in replacement for a worker who might be subjected to harsh working conditions better handled by a machine. Computerized controls on assembly lines, in chemical reactors, or at a construction site can allow for more precise performance of the production step, leading to higher quality in the end product, lower production costs, or higher productivity. Manufacturing engineers, mechanical engineers, and others have been at the forefront of converting industrial production from a practice requiring brute force and intensive labor to one that involves computer skills and judgment.

A good example of more intelligent manufacturing is a type of analysis of manufacturing processes known as statistical process control (SPC). When mass-production factories are in operation, it is common for the output to be examined by quality control experts to make sure that the products meet their specifications and do not vary significantly from one batch to the next. In the past this was done after the products were made. Learning from the Japanese, however (and such American experts as W. Edward Deming), manufacturers realized that it is much more effective to monitor quality while the products are being made rather than afterward. And the best way to do this is to apply the mathematics of statistics to the production process, measuring variations—no matter how minute—in each product and making sure that something that is only slightly off-spec now doesn't become seriously out of spec at a later point. Thus, statistical process control.

To run SPC properly, large amounts of data must be gathered rapidly on a variety of product characteristics. This data must be compared, and calculations must be made as to variations. Then a manufacturing manager must pinpoint problem areas and see to it that the problems are resolved. All of this must happen quickly, while production is ongoing, so that final product quality is maintained at a high level. Such an application calls for computers in large numbers.

But the problem is more complex than simply positioning many computers throughout the factory floor and pouring in production data. Elaborate software programs must be available to automate the steps of data-gathering and analysis. When a problem is encountered, the computer system must be able to isolate it and indicate what countermeasures should be taken. Finally, it is increasingly common for all the final product specifications to be delivered along with the product itself, especially in cases where the output of one manufacturer (a steel company, for example) goes to another manufacturer (such as an appliance supplier). There are new national and international standards to be met in supplying these data.

The bottom line for engineers and scientists is that there are plenty of high-tech opportunities for supplying these programs and computerized analyses for even decidedly low-tech forms of manufacturing. Some technologists are employed by the manufacturers themselves; others are employed by consulting organizations that are hired by the manufacturers for their expertise.

WHO WORKS WITH AUTOMATION TECHNOLOGIES?

Industrial engineering is one profession whose employment prospects are dramatically affected by automation technology. It used to be that industrial engineers were employed primarily to figure out the most efficient use of human labor by measuring, for example, how long it took a worker to perform a certain task. Today, however, the industrial engineer looks at the total manufacturing process.

Another specialized profession that influences factory automation and quality control is called operations research. Operations researchers are trained to analyze complex tasks with sophisticated mathematical techniques. The profession originated in the needs of the military during World War II to figure out the best ways to provide armed forces in the field with supplies. In peacetime, it was applied to the needs of airlines (which have to make sure that airplanes are in the right locations at all times), telecommunications systems, and ultimately, factories. As with the industrial engineer, the computer is an essential tool for the operations researcher.

Along with new attention being paid to how factory operations are organized and run, high-tech workers are also examining typical manufacturing processes to uncover improvements. These include such basic tasks as bending or cutting metal with complex machine tools. Metal can be cut or joined by hot torches (or welding machines); the use of high-temperature plasma torches is one example of how a traditional operation has been updated. (A plasma is a stream of hot, electrically charged matter; the sun, for example, is mostly plasma.)

In the early 1980s robotics captured the attention of the public and manufacturing researchers alike. A robot is essentially a computer-controlled device that carries out a complex task. Robotics has been under continual development for more than forty years, but still sees steady advancements. (In fact, along the way the term *robotics* has fallen out of favor, as the technology has evolved simply into computerized machinery.) Robotics continues to be important, and a considerable number of mechanical and electrical engineers, along with computer scientists, are employed in developing and using robots.

ELECTRONIC MATERIALS

The microelectronic applications of materials technology are possibly the most exciting development of all. We have grown accustomed to seeing the luminescent displays of digital watches, which have been around for about twenty-five years. We are beginning to grow accustomed to so-called liquid crystal displays, such as are seen on many laptop personal computers and pocket televisions. Researchers in the United States, Europe, and the Far East are competing furiously to win business in producing larger, better performing, yet cheaper flat-panel displays for television, computer projectors, and instrument panels. What had been a research concept a decade ago (a large but inexpensive liquid-crystal panel) is now a multibillion-dollar business.

That development could make watching soap operas from bed more convenient, but it could also help us in many more meaningful ways. A hospital could depend on such displays to help doctors and nurses monitor patients and to call up a patient's medical records quickly and easily. It could also improve the efficiency of television and video technology used in classrooms.

Another microelectronic compound that depends on new materials technologies is gallium arsenide (a bonding of the elements gallium and arsenic), which has certain superior properties for the manufacture of microchips, polymer plastics that can conduct electricity, and the components of magnets and batteries.

R&D IN MATERIALS AND PROCESSES

Who is carrying out all the R&D on new materials and processes? The answer depends on the specific application. In advanced metals and ceramics the aerospace industry is the leader. Aerospace companies have explored all kinds of exotic metallurgies in the search for materials that can be used in high-speed, high-temperature jet turbines. They are also at the forefront of devising ultralight, yet ultrastrong structures because every pound that a craft decreases in weight translates into higher speed or better fuel efficiency. These aerospace firms hire materials scientists and mechanical and metallurgical engineers to carry out the research.

The electronics applications of materials involve a wide range of companies, including small entrepreneurial outfits that are the brainchildren of one or two scientists as well as the mighty computer and electronics manufacturers. Warm superconductors were first conceived at an IBM laboratory, and IBM has already succeeded in commercializing at least one electronic application of them.

There are about 120,000 chemical engineers, chemists, and materials scientists employed in the United States today. The great majority of them work for major manufacturing companies, either in an R&D role or as managers that oversee production lines and project work. The overall outlook for employment is cloudy, as many materials companies have transferred a significant amount of their production capacity abroad to take advantage of lower labor rates and proximity to raw materials or inexpensive energy. However, much of the research work continues in North America, where the most advanced laboratories and concentrations of trained researchers exist.

CHAPTER 6

BIOTECHNOLOGY

Technology forecasters like to say that the last one hundred years was the century of the electron (as in electricity, electronics, and computers); this one will be the century of the gene, as in genetic engineering, genomics, and biotechnology.

There's no question that biotechnology has been taking up more and more newspaper headlines in the past few decades. From controversies over genetically modified foods, to stem cell research, to genetic screening of unborn children and others, or DNA sampling as a means of criminal and other government investigations, the power of new genetic and biotech knowledge multiplies every day.

Biotech is also a well-established, dynamic industry. Revenues in the United States for publicly traded biotech companies hit nearly $50 billion in 2005, according to an annual survey by the accounting firm Ernst & Young. In Canada, it reached nearly $2.6 billion. There were 1,415 U.S. companies and 459 Canadian ones in that year.

Biotech, to use the colloquial term, arose in the 1970s out of the development of a series of unrelated techniques to examine and manipulate the basic genetic material of life. Two decades before, during the 1950s, biologists James Watson and Francis Crick verified the double-helix structure of deoxyribonucleic acid (DNA), which is the chemical name for basic genetic material. The fascinating thing about DNA is its combined simplicity and complexity. It is simple in that it is composed of only six subcomponents— a sugar molecule, a phosphate molecule, and four nitrogen compounds (adenine, thiamine, guanine, and cytosine). The sugar and phosphates form a backbone chain, and the four nitrogen compounds are distributed along this backbone. That's it. All the complexity of life, from a puny weed to the cells in our brains, is written in the four nitrogen bases.

The brass ring for biotech research is unlocking and understanding the language and processes of human DNA. Another milestone was reached in 2000, when the human genome was mapped out in rough form by an international consortium led by the United States, along with a privately funded effort by a company called Celera Genomics. The sequencing was essentially completed in 2003. But human DNA is only one part of biotechnology. The techniques and knowledge gained in human genomics research has been rapidly conveyed into the agricultural arena, where agbiotech companies are developing refined versions of seed crops, enhancements to animal husbandry, and alterations of various crops harvested for industrial purposes. In reality, much of today's agbiotech simply builds on the cross-breeding and cultivation that have been practiced for centuries by farmers, but obviously the practice now has a much stronger scientific foundation. The practice is not without controversy—some European countries have banned genetically modified foods, and many individuals are not comfortable consuming such products. Agbiotech represents about 2 to 5 percent of the number of biotech companies in existence, but the output of its products is more valuable, as the seeds that an agbiotech company might sell become billions of bushels of wheat or corn each harvest.

A third component of the biotech revolution has come to be called industrial biotechnology. Like agbiotech, industrial biotech has a broad foundation of conventional cultivation of plant and animal resources, such as cotton, wool, leather, and other products. However, now molecular biology is pointing to the production of raw materials for chemical production, such as polylactide or propanediol, both of which can be used for plastics. Today the lion's share of attention in industrial biotechnology is shining on biomass-to-energy production, such as ethanol from corn for automotive fuel.

BIOPHARMACEUTICALS

While agbiotech and industrial biotech are very important within their arenas, the premier application for biotech is human health, primarily new medicines that are making a difference in age-old maladies such as cancer or heart disease, as well as some newer ones like AIDS.

The complexity of DNA arises from its miniscule size and the difficulty in transcribing this genetic code. DNA is millions of units long. Inside each cell, it resembles a tightly coiled snake. Simple chemical compounds are drawn out of the soup inside a cell and connected to each other according to the patterns defined by the four nitrogen bases. By the 1970s a new research discipline, molecular biology, had arisen to tease out the information encoded in DNA. Molecular biologists figured out how to make DNA replicate its instructions even when snipped from the original helix chain and transferred to another organism's DNA. Following another research path, molecular biologists succeeded in merging two cells together—one a cancerous tumor cell (which has the unwholesome property of never shutting off, but continuing to replicate), the other a cell that produces a valued antibody (antibodies are chemicals that protect an organism from bacterial attack or other forms of infection). By combining the two, a fused cell known as a hybridoma is produced. The hybridoma can produce the antibody practically without ever stopping. (As in all life, however, even a cell eventually dies.) These antibodies can be used to detect disease or even to combat it.

By about 1980 all the tools were in place for a veritable explosion of new biotechnology. Molecular biologists and biochemists were mixing many different types of DNA strands together, literally creating new forms of life. Antibodies that previously were obtained at fantastic expense and in minute supply could be produced in cookie-cutter fashion. Soon some drugs and diagnostic compounds worth hundreds of millions of dollars were being produced. Among the products that have successfully been commercialized are human growth hormone (to counter the effects of dwarfism), tissue plasimogen activator (a compound that helps heart attack victims), and interferon (a potential cancer fighter). Today, too, a woman can perform a pregnancy test quickly and inexpensively in her own home with a pregnancy test kit that has its roots in antibody R&D.

The latest sensation in biotech is stem cell research, which remains highly controversial due to its use of human embryos. Under the right conditions, stem cells have the amazing ability to become different functional parts of the human organism—nerve cells, muscle tissue (such as the heart), and perhaps even brain cells. They are being examined as medical therapies for spinal cord injuries (as famously espoused by the late Christopher Reeve), or for Alzheimer's disease, Parkinson's disease, and other maladies. They might be able to regenerate entire organs of the human body, without the rejection issues common to organ transplants.

Stem cells exist within us at all ages, and are also available at birth, from the umbilical cord, but scientists have found that the best starting material for stem cell research comes from human embryonic cells. And since, for many, embryonic cells are equivalent to human life, they are considered to be off-limits to experimentation. Scientists, bioethicists, and government officials are looking for a middle ground where stem cell research can continue with public funding; at present, most of the stem cell research going on in the United States is being done privately, without federal support.

Human biotechnology is a veritable cornucopia of new research methods, new diagnostic tools, and new ideas for therapies. This flood of high tech will continue for years to come.

BIOTECH WORKERS

The growth of biotechnology has caused some dramatic changes in curricula in many academic departments at colleges as new skills are sought by private industry. The study of biology as performed by cataloguing the variety of species and analyzing their differences and similarities has been overtaken by genetic methods for doing so. Now, most biology is genomics. Similarly, biochemistry has been transformed by molecular biology. At the engineering schools, biomedical engineering used to be an offshoot of chemical and mechanical engineering primarily devoted to human prosthetic devices. Now bioengineering has become a full-fledged engineering department of its own, concentrating on analytical and production techniques employing biotechnology.

Many of the larger biotech companies—or at least those that have made the transition from a research laboratory into one that manufactures biopharmaceuticals commercially—have the same structure as traditional pharmaceutical companies (and traditional pharma is looking more and more like biotech). Within the biopharmaceutical industry, however, the individual workers like to distinguish themselves from their traditional pharmaceutical brothers and sisters. But as time goes on, the two types of companies will resemble each other closely.

A large part of the workforce of traditional pharmaceutical businesses (and a growing part of biopharma) is dedicated to ensuring consistent quality of products and meeting regulatory reviews. The U.S. Food and Drug Administration is a large force in the operation of any type of pharmaceutical company; FDA inspectors and investigators routinely review operations and have the power to shut down operations or recall products from pharmacy shelves if quality has been compromised. Similarly, a large part of conducting pharmaceutical research is involved in clinical trials— meeting FDA standards for showing that a proposed new pharmaceutical is safe and effective. Clinical trial operations are themselves a multibillion-dollar, global industry (increasingly, clinical trials are being held outside the United States, in part because it is becoming more difficult to find candidates to participate in the trials who are not already using some other pharmaceutical products).

The drug discovery part of biotech primarily involves research scientists and medical specialists. When a candidate drug compound is identified, clinical trials are managed by medical professionals, nurses, and statisticians. After a drug has been tested and approved by the FDA, chemists, biologists, and engineers are involved in ramping up production. At every step along this path, numerous analytical chemists, instrumentation technicians, and medical test professionals are involved.

Biopharmaceutical products are geared toward human health and needs. A similar revolution is brewing in plant and animal science, where age-old diseases are being combated and where new, hardier crops are being developed. Historically, plant and animal scientists could develop a better crop or farm animal only by patiently crossing and recrossing breeds of them to bring forth new generations of life forms with the desired properties. Now, by manipulating genetic material, these properties can be targeted and expressed directly and quickly.

A variety of new professions have arisen due to the emergence of biotechnology. Many of these are at the leading edges of biological research. For instance, molecular biologists are able to analyze genetic material molecule by molecule and to manipulate the genetic material with other chemicals. The types of biotechnological applications that are emerging call for specialization even within molecular biology. There are protein chemists and biologists (proteins make up our muscles and tissues; DNA is also a protein);

enzymologists (enzymes control body chemistry); endocrinologists (who focus on hormones); immunologists (the immune system of the body combats illness); and virologists (who work with viruses). The dreadful loss of life caused by the AIDS virus over the past decades has intensified the search for new biotechnological answers, including a vaccine for the disease.

The recent history of biotechnology is not one of uniform success. Many companies tried and failed to commercialize techniques that either didn't produce the desired result or were felt to be too risky. In addition, the early forecasts of cranking out large volumes of hormones or other biochemicals for human use by genetically engineering bacteria have been tempered by the realization that many biochemicals have levels of complexity that scientists were only dimly aware of. The three-dimensional structure of biochemicals is an example of this; it is not enough to make a chemical with all the right molecules in a row; this chemical must also have the right spatial arrangement in order to function properly in the human body.

Still, thousands of biologists, biochemists, food and agriculture scientists, and others have joined the hundreds of new companies that have arisen in the past fifteen years to commercialize biotechnology. Year by year, the list of products that have been introduced lengthens, and more will come.

7

MEDICAL TECHNOLOGY AND HEALTH CARE

Health care is one of the biggest areas of economic activity in modern society, and for many years public and private expenditures for health care have risen much faster than the economy as a whole, which means that its dominance will only increase. Roughly $1.7 trillion was spent on health care in the United States in 2004; employment is in the millions.

An area of economic activity so vast as this is going to have many different occupations, areas of rapid growth or shrinkage, highly profitable sectors, or marginal or unprofitable ones. Being so large, the health-care industry is also influenced by national policies. The notable trends here are additional support for the elderly, especially as the baby boom generation approaches retirement age; increased support for pharmaceutical treatment of illnesses, as evidenced by the adoption of the Medicare Part D program to fund most of the drug costs of the elderly; and an ongoing debate over how much of health-care costs should come from government, how much from the individual, and how much from employers, who fund health care as part of their benefits packages for employees.

When we think of health care, we mostly think of doctors, hospitals, and nurses. There is, of course, much more to the health-care system. The raw materials, so to speak, of health care are medicines and pharmaceuticals, medical devices, and medical facilities. There is a large service component to health care: these are the doctors, nurses, technicians, facility workers, and administrators. Surrounding these are the funding sources: insurance companies, government agencies, private charities, and the individual consumer. This view of health care is itself in question as an industrial model; another way of looking at health care starts with individual wellness and focuses on nutrition, exercise, and lifestyle choices, then moves outward to the services individuals might need, such as doctors or hospitals. The point here is that different philosophies of health care imply different types of services.

A common element to both the industrial perspective on health care and the wellness perspective is information and education. Most health-care professionals have clinical work as a significant part of their training, meaning that they learn on the job. The use of teaching hospitals is a widespread practice. Similarly, as individuals, we are becoming more energetic consumers of health-care information. Health programs are now a common component of television programming. The Internet is creating new communication channels for disseminating health-care information.

There are high-tech aspects to all of this activity. In this section, we'll focus on the more prominent ones: pharmaceuticals and biotechnology, medical devices, and health information.

PHARMACEUTICALS AND BIOTECHNOLOGY

Within the past generation, a revolution has occurred in mental health care. Because of a better understanding of brain chemistry, a prominent part of the practice of psychiatry is now deciding what drugs to dispense, rather than what type of Freudian talking cure to engage in or what type of group therapy to participate in. In truth, the best mental health care programs partake of both activities, but the initial resistance of the mental health professions to the use of pharmaceuticals has mostly been overwhelmed by the success of new drugs to help handle depression, psychosis, and other problems.

That trend is but one example of how significantly pharmaceuticals have moved into all aspects of health care. Some people worry about America being an overmedicated society; on the other hand, it is often the case that one can take a drug instead of having a surgical procedure, or instead of compromising the quality of one's life when a long-term illness such as diabetes or heart disease is present.

The pharmaceutical industry has more than a century of scientific research into the chemistry and physiology of the human body, and that body of knowledge stands on millennia of sometimes helpful, sometimes harmful folk knowledge. Within the past generation, however, the entire field has taken a dramatic new direction as a result of new genetic information. The unlocking of the human genome (DNA), along with related developments in the study of cellular mechanisms, has led to the development of drugs synthesized from microbial "factories," to diagnostic tests that can identify an illness at a very early stage (and therefore more amenable to treatment), and to various drugs that are tied directly to the biochemical activities that occur in our organs.

It used to be that pharmaceutical research was an organized activity, but with an uncertain outcome: new compounds would be thought of, tested for physiological effects on mice or guinea pigs, and then, if some promise showed, tested on humans. Now the pattern is to probe deeply into the structure and actions of individual cells and to create a medicine using genetic manipulations of bacteria or other living cells to produce a candidate drug.

From 1996, not long after the first genetically engineered drugs were commercialized, to 2006, the pharmaceutical industry has more than tripled in sales volume. In 2005 new drug applications via biotechnology exceeded those from conventional biochemistry for the first time. This trend will continue to intensify as more experience is gained with the new tools made available by biotechnology.

MEDICAL DEVICES

In a fashion similar to the growth and advances in pharmaceuticals and genetics, researchers and enterprising companies have vastly expanded the variety and capabilities of medical devices for health care. Medical devices cover a broad spectrum from the diagnostic tools that doctors use, such as CAT (computerized axial tomography) or MRI (magnetic resonance imaging) machines that provide views of the inner workings of the human body, to tools that surgeons or doctors use on the operating table, to prosthetic devices such as artificial limbs, heart valves, or whole organs.

In stark contrast to many other industries, the medical device industry is characterized by a large number of small, entrepreneurially driven companies. According to data gathered by the International Trade Administration (an office of the U.S. Department of Commerce), there were approximately eight thousand medical device companies in 2001, but 80 percent of them have fifty or fewer employees. The biggest companies are, in fact, very big and dominate the revenues of the industry, but while some of them are well known, such as GE Medical Systems, Johnson & Johnson, and Abbot Laboratories, others are not so well known: Guidant, Stryker Corp., and Tyco Healthcare.

According to U.S. Bureau of Labor Statistics data, there were about three hundred thousand workers in this field in 2005. The overall value of the medical device industry is about $80 billion, and the industry is very successful in generating exports (the volume of imports, however, is close to the value of exports). Growth rates vary from year to year, but have been well in excess of the U.S. economy as a whole.

Medical devices are a fascinating combination of traditional healthcare devices and the highest of high tech. Microchips and computers are being adapted to operate artificial limbs by thought (the systems depend on training other muscles in the amputee's body to generate a signal that causes the electromechanical parts in the artificial limb to move). Cardiologists and pharmaceutical scientists have joined together to develop stents—small tubes made of a metal mesh—that are coated with a drug and then inserted into the blocked arteries of heart-disease patients. In the biotech arena, scientists have developed ways to grow artificial skin or specialized cells from a patient's own body and then apply those to the patient to close a wound or repair an organ. Meanwhile, new technology steadily advances the capabilities of many traditional medical devices, such as dental implants, glasses or other vision assistance, hearing aids, and the like.

On a technological basis, medical devices are equally fascinating. The field requires a knowledge of medicine (how the human body operates), mechanical or electronics engineering, and a wide variety of more specialized bodies of knowledge depending on the application. The materials aspects of many medical devices call for an in-depth knowledge of materials science or chemical engineering.

How can you prepare for this field? With such a wide range of technologies involved, all of the disciplines mentioned are appropriate. Many of the most successful practitioners combine training in a technology (engineering, chemistry, physics) with a medical degree. Many schools now have departments of biotechnology or biomedical engineering, which are also relevant preparation.

Overall, the medical device industry will take advantage of the same economic forces that are driving all of North American health care: an aging population, a desire for more effective health care, and a need to control costs through more precise application of medicines or medical procedures. The entrepreneurial nature of the industry indicates that many businesspeople see new opportunities ahead.

HEALTH INFORMATION TECHNOLOGY

One would want to believe that, since our personal health is one of our most valuable possessions, the application of new technologies like computers or the Internet would have been rapidly taken up in the U.S. health-care system. Regrettably, this has not been the case. Most prescriptions are still handwritten by the doctor, and the piece of paper is carried by the patient to a pharmacy for the medicine to be dispensed. When we have a need to visit a new doctor, the first step is often to repeat all the same personal and medical information that was communicated at the previous doctor's visit. Hospitals spend inordinate amounts of time filling out, storing, and retrieving paper copies of health records.

The problems all this manual recordkeeping causes are well known, and many hospital administrators and health-care practitioners have attempted to address them. Nevertheless, it will be years before all the kinks have been worked out, and we are able to retain and make use of health records with the same ease with which financial records are maintained. One problem is how to address privacy issues: most Americans consider their personal health information to be very private and have supported privacy rules that prevent health information from being shared by different organizations. Another is, simply, tradition: if medical doctors are not required to, say, use a computer keyboard to fill out a prescription, they are inclined not to do so. A third factor is the complexity of health information, which ranges from volumes of numerical data from lab tests to the qualitative information of how we feel. A fourth factor is that, in many cases, the organization that is being called on to make an investment in new information technology has little incentive to do so because the savings of such an investment will benefit some other organization. For example, hospitals would like to invest in electronic health records to digitize patients' records, but one of the main beneficiaries of that investment would be the private insurance companies that compensate for health-care costs. (That particular situation has become so extreme that, in 2006, rules were established whereby insurance companies could pay the hospitals to install the equipment without running afoul of federal regulations.)

Winds of change are about to blow through the health-care system. Late in his first administration, President George W. Bush set up an Office of the National Coordinator for Health Information Technology (HIT). In 2006, the Health and Human Services Administration formed a group called the American Health Information Community, which will combine a variety of offices of the federal government with private industry contractors to develop a coordinated effort to address shortcomings in HIT.

A number of very exciting, very advanced technologies are being brought to bear on HIT. One is the use of digital imaging systems (digital x-rays, CAT scans) and the ability to transmit these images anywhere the Internet reaches. Using these technologies, medical specialists can make diagnoses of patients who might be across the continent. Such types of telemedicine have the potential to bring patients and the best medical specialists together without the need for travel.

Another example is the use of a combination of microelectronics and radio called radio frequency identification (RFID). Hospitals and pharmaceutical companies are concerned with what is called the continuum of care, meaning that there is a straightforward path from when the medicine is prescribed to when it is administered to a patient. Pharmacists, nurses, and other care providers must ensure that the right medication, in the right dose, is given to the right patient. By combining a radio chip on the pharmaceutical package with a similar device on the patient's wristband, a nurse, using a radio scanning device, can match the patient's identity with the medication.

RFID and telemedicine are two examples in which a new technology needs to be coordinated with the care practices of the hospital or health-care provider. Successful implementation of HIT requires knowledge of both technology and professional practices. This is a good example of the expertise of academic training in information technology or management of information systems, as opposed to computer science or engineering (see Chapter 14 for details on the distinctions between computer science and information technology).

The federal government, as well as health-care insurers, is stepping into the HIT shortfall being experienced by the health-care system. Modernization of HIT is expected to be a major force in reducing the dramatic increases in health-care costs that have occurred in recent years.

C H A P T E R

8

ELECTRONICS, COMPUTERS, AND COMMUNICATIONS

This chapter is about hardware; the next chapter, "Information Technology," will be about software and the Internet. Separating the two this way is somewhat old-fashioned; it is certainly true that in the early days of computing the hardware developers were in their own world; the programmers were thought to be little more than typists to send instructions into the early computers and record the results that came out. (And that is one of the reasons the first leaders of software development were often women; they had the experience of developing the programs that the computers ran.) In more recent years, hardware and software development have been intertwined; computer code is embedded in hardware to make it work properly; conventional computer and microelectronics design happens first in software-driven simulations, and then the design files are turned into physical circuits and electronic components to build the actual device.

Still, there remains a different culture and different kinds of expertise called on for developing electronic hardware versus software. Hardware designers have to deal with the physical constraints of metals, semiconductors, and input/output devices. Software developers, by and large, deal with the complexities of logic, the various languages that computer programs can be written in, and the need to translate abstract business or work-related functions into the steps of a computer program, or the output desired from an electronic device like a video screen, or a digital packet conveyed down a communications line. Somewhat confusing to the uninformed outsider, developers of digital content ranging from high-definition movies to animated websites have taken to calling their output software, as if the mere practice of converting a video clip or piece of text into digital information were a form of computer programming.

MOORE'S LAW

Perhaps the central, unifying theme of how electronic hardware has evolved is Moore's Law, named after Gordon Moore, one of the founders of Intel Corporation. Moore's Law, which exists only as a paraphrase of a point Moore was making about the pace with which transistors could be crammed onto microchips, said that the transistor density would double every eighteen to twenty-four months, while the product cost would remain roughly the same. Other advances in electronics, such as the speed of access or density of storage on a magnetic disk, or the communication speed across a network, have been shown to have similar evolutions (faster in some cases, slower in others). Moore's simple statement has several profound implications:

- Microelectronic capabilities will continuously advance, becoming faster, bigger, and/or cheaper under current conditions. This is the source of one of the irritations of buying computerized equipment: if you wait a bit, it will inevitably be cheaper, and in the meantime an improved product will also appear.
- Companies in the microelectronic hardware business will have to adapt to continuously declining prices and to continually advancing technical capabilities. There's no chance for a company to develop a great product, put it on the market, and then simply sell it for several years. The product will have to be continuously improved, and its price will have to drop.
- As the price of microelectronic equipment gets lower, its applicability continually broadens. Even in the early days of the personal computer (let alone the even more distant days of mainframe computing), if you had told someone that computers would get so cheap and easy to use that most public libraries would have them available to patrons, or that they would be sitting in hotel lobbies, classrooms, and homes, you would have been thought to be crazy. Furthermore, today's cell phones are more and more

like handheld computers, while actual handheld computers (personal digital assistants) have sprouted Internet or telephonic connections. The cheaper technology creates gigantic new markets for software and communication services.

These larger markets lead to another basic principle of computers and communications: the network effect, where the value of a network rises exponentially as more and more users join it. A communications channel between two people is great, but a conversation between a blogger and thousands of readers of that blog, together with the blogs that they themselves might maintain, creates an entire subculture.

MICROELECTRONICS

There are so many types of microelectronic devices, for so many different applications, that any sort of comprehensive list of them would look like a telephone book. But there are some broad classes of devices to consider:

- **Sensors.** Sensors are input devices; they react in some physically measurable form to a stimulus such as light, sound, or electromagnetic signals and themselves generate a signal, usually digital, that gets sent to a central data-collection unit.
- **Processing units.** Processing units range from simple switches that take some action when receiving a signal, to the integrated circuit "brains" of computers, audio or television equipment, factory controls, and so on. Although lots of attention is paid to the latest Pentium or IBM chip being used in a computer, millions more such chips are used in humdrum electronic equipment ranging from calculators to thermostats. Today's automobiles have about a dozen processors on board, controlling everything from the car's interior air conditioning to the fuel-air ratio inside the engine.
- **Communication and networking equipment.** Communication ranges from a piece of wire along which a signal is sent to the Internet "pipes" that carry terabytes of data packets from continent to continent. Sophisticated methods of compiling the data signals through routers or digital switches are necessary parts of most networks. Converting the electrical signals into optical signals

vastly improves transmission speed. Going in another direction, more and more communication is occurring wirelessly, involving radio transmitters and receivers and satellites. At the other end of the data-transmission scale, it is now becoming more commonplace to include a radio frequency identification (RFID) chip on credit cards, consumer packaged goods, or personal ID tags; these chips only send a signal when a transmitter in their vicinity energizes them, allowing a kilobyte or so of data to be uploaded.

- **Data storage.** Hard drives, flash memory, CD-ROMs, DVDs, magnetic tape, holographic memory devices, data warehouses, server farms . . . the ways in which data can be stored increase in size and variety. Once information, ranging from an optical scan of a page of a paper-based book to the optical images recorded by an interplanetary probe, can be digitized, it can be stored on many varieties of media.

- **Human interface devices.** A computer chip inside, say, an automobile does not normally interact with the driver; what it does might be completely invisible to the driver. But most types of consumer electronics, computers, and many other devices act either to receive a command from a human operator or to provide an output to a human. Computers have video screens and keyboards; cell phones have audio speakers as well as screens; DVD players link to television screens so that we can enjoy high-resolution views of the latest movies. In the early days of computerization, people spoke of the paperless office, little realizing how much ink and paper would be consumed by computer printers, another human interface device. The switch from tubular screens to flat panels is a recent example of how this area of electronics evolves. Prognosticators say that we're heading for digital paper, in which a think sheet would display this morning's newspaper or the novel we happen to be reading.

All of these developments depend on highly complex applications of solid-state physics, circuit design, data storage and switching, and many other areas of expertise. And yet, especially for consumer electronics, the designs come together in a rush and are offered to the marketplace seemingly overnight, and then are rendered obsolete by next year's designs and more powerful components. Moore's Law is still very much in effect.

The typical semiconductor fab (short for "fabrication line")—a microchip factory—can cost more than $1 billion or more to build these days, and the price continues to rise. This aspect of the microelectronics industry is not as widely recognized as the output of these fab lines, but there is a comparable rate of technological advancement in the fabrication machinery for chips and components. Here we enter the arena of optical lithography, chemical vapor deposition, molecular beam epitaxy, ion implantation, and other esoteric production methods. The dominant trend affecting microelectronic fabrication is the continual shrinkage of the dimensions of the features (components) on a chip. The current state of the art is around 90 nanometers, but already chips are appearing with 65-nm features. The smaller the dimensions, the more components can be crammed onto a chip and, within a variety of physical limitations, the shorter the distance a signal has to travel from one component to the next.

There are several well-defined job functions in the microelectronics world, and dozens of less well-defined ones. This is partly because, as the technology rapidly advances, new types of occupations are created, and some older ones reduced or eliminated. The main jobs are materials and electronics research, integrated circuit (IC) design, product design, microelectronics fabrication or manufacture, and test and assembly.

Materials research can be blue-sky basic research or, since the future goals of many types of microelectronics design are well understood, the applied research to figure out how to make new microelectronics. These researchers work in laboratories, with small fab systems in place to test out new ideas.

When a new type of microelectronics material or capability is figured out, IC designers must figure out how to build it into the design of a microchip. The innovation might necessitate use of new materials or a new way to carve out or build up the features of a chip. There are highly specialized software programs that assist chip designers in this task; it is said that it is now impossible for one person to keep track of all of the features of a chip, so that chip design must be done with automated tools.

With a chip design in place, the manufacturing engineers go to work. Interestingly, a microelectronics fab looks very much like a laboratory, since the production machinery consists of large, complex devices that need multiple operators, and the production goes on in sterile, filtered-air "clean rooms" with workers encased in head-to-toe space suits. (One inopportune sneeze could ruin a highly valuable production batch; thus the need for ultraclean operating conditions.) The challenge for most fab managers is to figure out how to reduce the error rate (a bad batch of chips) from 50 percent or more for each production run down to a few percentage points. Since the production processes are labor-intensive and expensive, each percentage point improvement in yield (the proportion of good product) can be worth millions of dollars per day.

With new chips coming onto the market, or with new electronic devices such as flat-panel screens or miniature cameras becoming available, product designers can go to work. The challenge is to figure out the right combination of new and conventional components to make a final assembled product that will be commercially successful. The Apple iPod is an obvious example; the product's success is in part due to use of new, very small data storage devices that allow thousands of songs to be stored in a small, handheld device, combined with small yet strong power storage batteries that allow the device to be free of a power cord.

Test and assembly is a critical but poorly recognized part of electronics manufacture. Electronic products contain hundreds or thousands of individual components. If manufacturers simply assembled all these components and then tested for desired performance, it is doubtful that a new cell phone or DVD player would ever reach the market. Rather, testing must be built into the production process at many intermediate steps so that flaws can be isolated and resolved before they affect the rest of the assembled product. Testing and assembly involves sophisticated statistical analysis of production data to uncover errors, the use of software simulation to run a device or component through its paces prior to inclusion in the larger assembly, and analytical equipment to find out if a flaw occurs because of physical imperfections in the components. Being able to isolate and minimize production flaws rapidly can be the difference between a successful electronics manufacturer and a failing one.

COMPUTERS

Microchip design is a key part of the electronic hardware industry and a good metaphor for the characteristics of all microelectronics manufacturing. At the other end of the microchip scale—where hundreds or thousands of them are assembled—there is another good metaphor for large electronic projects: the supercomputer. While supercomputing is not a large market, the capabilities of supercomputing often define the leading edge of where all computing eventually goes. It has often been said that today's midrange personal computer easily exceeds the capabilities of behemoth supercomputers of a decade or so ago; looking forward, today's supercomputing capabilities will be the pattern for future personal computers.

Computers, whether personal or for supercomputing, used to be readily identifiable as distinct products, generally seen in blandly colored metal boxes on a desk or in a room. There are still many such devices to be found in offices, in homes, or being carried by business executives. The introduction of a new computer model used to be a signal event, with considerable media hoopla over the new technology and capabilities incorporated into the machine. New computers are continually being developed, but these days it tends to be a more incremental step, rather than an exciting, new dimension of technological capability. The current microprocessor chip at the heart of the computer might be changed out for a newer one; better, faster data storage or displays might be incorporated. These changes are expected.

Where computers are generating the most excitement is at the very small end—various types of handheld PCs, smartphones, or personal digital assistants (PDAs)—and at the very large end—supercomputing. Putting a computer in a handheld device is happening, mostly, because businesspeople want access to the data at corporate headquarters. At the consumer level, there is a strong push for various types of personal entertainment devices. Although most people don't think of it this way, the wildly successful Apple iPod is, in fact, a computer.

A supercomputer is simply the biggest, fastest computer at any given time. Around 1984, the first giga-FLOP (10^9 floating point operations per second, a measure of computer processing speed) was developed in the then-Soviet Union. In 1997, Intel developed the first tera-FLOP machine (one thousand times more powerful than a giga-FLOP machine). Currently, an IBM design known as Blue Gene holds the record, running at upwards of 280 tera-FLOPs. Meanwhile, over the past twenty years or so the concept of parallel computing—using multiple computers to work on a single problem simultaneously—has been established. These computer networks can also run in the tera-FLOPs range. The latest variation of parallel processing is known as grid computing and is based on the concept of having thousands of individual computers (which can be as small as home PCs) work on problems.

Giga-FLOPs, tera-FLOPs (and soon, peta-FLOPs)—what difference does this make in the scheme of things? Supercomputing allows very large problems to be worked on in a meaningful way, meaning that a conclusion to a problem is based on doing trillions of computing steps in a relatively short period of time. Some of the best-known problems are climate modeling (to get a better sense of the effects of global warming), conventional weather forecasting (which can be extremely data-intensive), lots of hush-hush U.S. military operations, petroleum exploration, DNA analysis, and many more. The Council on Competitiveness, a Washington, D.C.–based advocacy group, is trying to build support for expanding the network of supercomputer centers nationally so that supercomputing can be brought into the more conventional realms of mechanical design, health research, and other commercial areas.

Through the early 1990s, supercomputer manufacture and software development were dynamic, growing businesses for a small number of companies. Declining costs of microprocessors and the development of parallel processing machines, which offer a low-cost alternative to the "big iron" of a supercomputer, have tackled many of the types of problems that supercomputing was targeting. There are technical issues with parallel processing, though, having to do with the ability to chop a computer program into many small pieces that can be performed simultaneously on multiple computers. The supercomputing realm is not as dynamic as it once was, but it still represents the leading edge of computing capability.

In terms of jobs, supercomputing attracts mathematicians and computer science specialists who can address the parallel-processing issue. Only a handful of companies are building the machines (including IBM, Fujitsu, Intel, and a few others).

The overall computer equipment market is about $115 billion annually, according to data cited by the U.S. Department of Commerce. An additional $80 billion is spent on computer software. The revenues of companies that provide information services based on computers adds another $150 billion. This brings the total to about $350 billion, and the number grows rapidly from year to year. At least one million workers are employed in computer manufacture, software development, and computerized information services.

As these figures indicate, there is at least as much money, if not more, spent on the use of computers as on their manufacture. This has been true for many years. The typical concept has been of a young person eager to work in computers becoming a computer designer or manufacturer, preferably at an industry leader such as IBM. Yet an equally high-tech career can be found in producing information via computers, from the daily financial data that Wall Street depends on to the CD-ROM disks that provide the text of a report or book at the user's desktop.

The computer industry sometimes reminds one of Texans, who are famous for bragging about nearly anything. Case in point: most businesses are happy to grow consistently at a rate slightly above the overall growth in the gross national product (GNP), a measure of the size of the overall economy. In most years, that rate would be in the range of 4 to 8 percent. Computer manufacturers, on the other hand, consider any growth rate below 10 percent to be a slump. For example, a couple of years ago David Kearns, then chairman of Xerox Corporation, was interviewed by the *Wall Street Journal.* He "leaves no doubt that [the company will] return to the double-digit growth rates it last saw in the mid-1980s, 'rather than dinking along at 6 percent or 7 percent.'"

COMMUNICATIONS EQUIPMENT

Like the transition to smaller and smaller chip features that drives microelectronics manufacture, the individuals and companies that build communications equipment know very clearly what they are going to be doing for the next several years: developing servers, routers, and switching equipment that will expand the volume of data flowing into home and office computers. There are already big data "pipes" connecting regions or continents; large telephone and networking companies also have these pipes to connect cities or corporate centers. The problem has been the "last mile," connecting, say, a local telephone hub into the home or small office.

What everyone wants is cheap, fast broadband access, such that videos can be streamed into the home or telephone calls can routinely include video as well as audio components. Some of this demand might also be met by wide-area high-fidelity (Wi-Fi) connections, and some cities are seeking to install these connections as a municipal service. The United States is behind other nations in this effort, notwithstanding the fact that this country has the largest number of computer users.

Communications and networking are their own scientific and engineering specialties. Backgrounds in electrical or electronic engineering or in computer science are common.

Today's communications equipment looks very much like computer hardware. The telephone companies have large boxes, or digital switches, that handle the routing of a call from one station to another. Similar systems handle the network of cellular phones blanketing the world; the main difference is that the switching equipment gathers calls from, and routes them to, radio transmitters instead of the copper wires that are the medium for landlines.

The Internet, of course, has brought profound change to communications. Once information—words, pictures, video, sound, instrument signals, and more—is digitized, it can be shipped via the Internet for distribution anywhere. Companies like Cisco and Juniper Networks have become giants by supplying the routing equipment and servers that convey digital information throughout the Internet.

Computer networking is an old-fashioned phrase referring to the technology that connects groups of computers to peripheral devices. Originally this occurred in one room; next, within one building, and then within a group of buildings that could be wired together either with copper or with some type of radio connection. With the Internet, computer networking is now merely one more manifestation of the Internet itself. The online communication you might be having at a given moment could be occurring through a computer on the other side of the world, or on the other side of a room; it mostly does not matter.

Advances in Internet or networking technology are driven by the desire for ever more chunks of data being delivered ever faster. Television via the Internet, for example, is just becoming to be broadly available; in the next few years, we can expect that most television will arrive via an Internet connection rather than over the airwaves. (Whether it is delivered by the telephone company, the cable TV company, or a cellular telephony network, however, remains to be seen.)

The communications hardware arena is sure to be an area of lively development, new inventions, and new jobs for the next several years.

CHAPTER

9

INFORMATION TECHNOLOGY

One of the most scandalous misperceptions about high-tech careers occurred during the period from 2001 to 2004, following the dot-com bust when many new Internet-related companies shut their doors, and when many of today's graduating college students were in high school and beginning to make decisions about future career paths. Because a significant number of information technology (IT) companies, including IBM, Microsoft, and others began opening R&D and employment centers in India, China, and other parts of Asia, the impression was created that North America's most valued high-tech jobs were being offshored to lower-cost countries and that IT would therefore be a bad career direction.

In fact, many North American companies were laying workers off, hiring in Asia, and trying to cut costs as the U.S. economy slowed. But what got lost in the headlines about offshoring is that high-tech industries—software development in particular—have always been a highly dynamic, unstable field for individuals and companies. New companies rise up, are absorbed by other companies, or decline and disappear at a stunning rate. Many IT workers have become accustomed to taking a job for a few years, working on several projects, and then moving on to other companies and other projects.

More to the point, IT professions, especially those involving R&D, are among the fastest-growing and highest demand of any careers in the United States today. U.S. employment in all types of programming, software, and networking jobs is expected to grow by 31.4 percent between 2004 and

2014, from just more than 3 million jobs to just more than 4 million. Certain specialties within the field—including software application engineers and data communications engineers—will grow by around 50 percent.

What is going on? The simple answer is to refer, again, to Moore's Law. As explained in the previous chapter, Moore's Law is a rule of thumb that predicts that computing power will double each eighteen to twenty-four months, without rising in cost. Moore's Law creates lots of challenges for computer hardware engineers, who seemingly have to run as hard as they can to stay in place with successful, stable businesses; one delay or false move, and the time spent recovering could mean the death of a company that misses a transition from one level of computing performance to the next.

But an interesting thing happens when Moore's Law is applied to software and applications—the world of IT workers. Because the cost of everything digital (microprocessors, data storage, communication rates) falls dramatically with each jump in computing performance, last year's impossibly expensive computing project becomes this year's trivial undertaking.

A simple example of this is the ability to put a movie on a DVD disk. Movies and video require large files (several megabytes) to be stored and replayed; if you had to spend ten thousand dollars to buy a specialized, high-speed data storage unit in the late 1990s just to play a twenty-dollar movie, you weren't going to buy that storage unit, or that DVD. But when a DVD player has become a hundred-dollar commodity electronics item (or, even less expensive, a DVD drive inside a laptop computer), you might buy many movies. You might even use a digital video camera (whose prices are also falling), make your own movie, post it on a public website, and wait for the acclaim from film fans. What makes all this possible is that more powerful yet less expensive computer hardware creates new markets or job opportunities for computer software.

In a broader context, as the cost of gathering data and writing application programs to do something to that data falls, businesses and individuals are willing to take on new tasks that seemed nearly impossible a few years prior. The idea, for example, of using supercomputers to analyze weather patterns and therefore predict tomorrow's weather or the effects of global climate change, or the ability to animate characters in a 3-D simulacrum—would have been fantastical a decade ago. Today they are high-school science projects. In other words, new IT hardware makes new IT applications grow.

What are the current hot spots of opportunity and business growth in IT? There are plenty to choose from:

- **Economic modeling and financial planning.** For years now, some of the best-paying jobs in IT have been with Wall Street investment banks that use IT to develop new ways to model complex financial transactions or make market forecasts. The so-called quants (quantitative analysts) use advanced mathematical models, combined with mountains of market data and historical patterns, to ferret out new market insights.
- **Business data warehouses.** The practice of consumer-goods companies of collecting information on who buys their products, and why, predates computers and information technology but has taken on radically new dimensions in recent years. Today it is becoming increasingly common for businesses to compile vast amounts of digital data and then to perform statistical analyses to understand what is going on within their business. By collecting this data almost in real time (as events happen) from such locations as the electronically connected cash registers at retail stores, business managers are able to make better decisions in managing inventories, initiating new production runs, adjusting prices, and predicting corporate financial performance. The success of the retail giant Wal-Mart—now the largest corporation in the world in terms of annual sales—has been widely attributed to its close management of sales data, which enables it to undercut the prices of competitors and thereby win consumer loyalty.
- **Genetics and personalized medicine.** Primarily through the use of advanced computing methods, the human genome was cracked in 2003 (see also Chapter 6). Now medical researchers are sifting individuals' personal genetic data to find appropriate medications, to predict future health conditions, or to repair physical damage. The genetics part of this activity is commonly known as bioinformatics, and it is a strong growth area for pharmaceutical companies, health-care providers, and researchers. On a parallel path, the entire modern health-care system, both in the United States and in other advanced industrial nations, is shifting to a more

evidence-based methodology, whereby decisions on treatment proceed on the basis of statistical analysis of past practices. This has been done sporadically by hospitals or medical professionals in the past, but now promises to be more rigorously—and successfully—applied in the future, as more health data are gathered, analyzed, and validated.

- **Geology and geophysics.** For the past generation, one of the most aggressive consumers of high-powered computers and specialized software has been the major oil-exploration companies, which have used computational systems to analyze underground geologic conditions to predict where petroleum resources are located. The process combines knowledge of geological strata with computational visualization tools and with data generated from soundings, exploratory wells, and other observable conditions. Now the same tools are being applied to managing water resources, to hunting for other types of minerals, and to such challenges as earthquake prediction.

- **Climate modeling.** At least in research circles, the debate over global warming has died down; it is now accepted science that humanity's activities are having an effect on the global climate. The questions are now shifting to making predictions of the effects of climate change, and designing systems either to prepare for these effects, or to counter global warming with some type of corrective action. For meteorologists and climatologists, there will be a need for better IT systems and software programs to analyze these effects and actions. Year by year, the ability of meteorologists to predict next week's weather gets better refined. Several private companies have been formed in recent years to provide seasonal weather forecasts to private customers, such as investment companies that need to make projections of weather conditions for agriculture, insurance, energy consumption, and other societal trends for business purposes.

Another, different sort of data collection and analysis can be grouped under the general term *digital entertainment*. As consumers, we have all become accustomed to watching digitized movies, while surrounded by digital sound systems, on (the latest trend) high-definition digital television sets. At the same time, a hobby that is fast becoming an avocation for individuals is to digitally record anything of interest (sports events, playing a guitar in one's bedroom) and upload the digital file onto a website for sharing with friends or the world. It is now commonplace in Hollywood and other entertainment capitals to speak of these recordings as "software"—the digitized information that can then be packaged as DVDs, subscription websites, or evening television and sold. Strictly speaking, these recordings are not software, but merely data files. But in the context of matching digital information with purchases of that information, the recordings become an information technology product that takes on many of the same attributes as computer programs.

An even more apt example is the newest massive multiuser video games, in which thousands of game players join online to enact battles, build virtual cities, or engage in other simulated games. Individually, these games are billion-dollar properties for their developers; collectively, they dwarf the dollar value of the global movie industry. And yet, at their core, they are computer programs that interact with users in ways that are similar to how in the past a computer programmer might have built a program to plot mathematical data. Another fascinating twist to these multiuser games is that it is now possible to earn revenue by selling attributes of the game won by their players (such as the superior status that comes from having won battles or built valuable virtual locations), meaning that the virtual game environment now can have as much economic value as a job in the real world. Is this computer programming? Is it entertainment?

This list of applications is merely a sampling of what is current as of the middle of the first decade of the twenty-first century. Give the scene a few years, and different ones will rise up—the IT field is that dynamic.

JOB TITLES

It is hard to summarize all the aspects of information technology that translate into actual businesses or jobs. But, measured by the volume of data generated, information technology has scaled upward by orders of magnitude in recent years. Measured by the value of digital content or information, it is in the trillions of dollars and rising rapidly. Measured by employment, it is roughly three million jobs in the United States today, and projected to rise to four million in a decade.

Traditionally, IT jobs were organized either around computers and hardware (see Chapter 8), programming (writing actual programs), and data entry (getting information digitized and then into a computer, or back out as readable text). As computers became more complex, and as methods to interconnect computers arose, the profession of systems analyst arose. Part of the task of systems analysts is to ensure that sufficient computing resources are on hand to run the programs that the programmers have written. On the information systems side, data entry quickly became more complicated methods of collecting and verifying digital information, and the profession came to be known as management of information systems (MIS). In the business world, at least, MIS now has a considerable degree of complexity, as organizations deal with steadily advancing requirements for financial reporting, accurate recordkeeping, forecasting, and operations. Somewhere between the user orientation of MIS departments and the systems orientation of an IT department is another specialized area called database administration. Database administrators combine a network systems outlook with the nature and requirements of large databases, with the goal of ensuring that the data are stored correctly and can be retrieved as needed. An area of growing concern to all of these functions—MIS, database administration, software engineering, and systems and network analysis—is computer security.

With the growth of the Internet, and with the continuing advances in computer technology (remember Moore's Law), the topic of network communications has arisen, and now plays a critical role in the successful operation of IT systems. If, for example, you had to put in a request for a cash withdrawal at a bank ATM and then come back an hour later to get your money, you probably would not be using ATMs very frequently. But networking technology has enabled banking systems to receive your request, confirm the availability of your funds, and produce the cash literally within seconds.

The Internet has also had another, more subtle effect on computer technology. Computer programs are being written now that can be used remotely from where data is stored, so that the computer processing (the running of the program) can occur separately from data entry and retrieval. Consider the operation of an Internet search engine: it continually scrolls through the content of websites on the Internet, finding and storing information on topics. When you type in a search request on Google, the program doesn't troll through the entire Internet, looking for your search terms; rather, it retrieves the information it has already collected and presents that to you. The Internet has had a profound effect on how computer programs are written and how they operate. This aspect of IT is both network administration and software development, and the ongoing revolution in IT caused by the Internet is putting those two professions in high demand.

In terms of educational preparation, IT jobs run the gamut from those that only need a high school diploma all the way to doctoral degrees. The lower-paying jobs (and those with lower educational requirements) are more concerned with moving data around, such as data entry clerks and records retrieval clerks. The highest levels are concerned with new ways to process data—mathematical simulations, computer languages, statistical methods of abstracting data. The middle ground is occupied by network administrators, systems administrators, programmers, and software engineers. Another trend, perhaps unique to IT, is that new information systems continually turn jobs into products. Data entry as an occupation has declining demand today, because so much data entry can now be automated. (The most extreme example of this might be Google, again, which is in the process of digitizing the world's libraries. Robotic machines and optical character recognition systems make the task nearly completely automatic.) Even computer programming is becoming automated; there are computer programs that are used to write computer programs. What keeps more and more IT workers employed, though, is that as new types of IT are developed, new demands for even better or faster IT systems follow right along.

A last important aspect of the IT world is that, while academic education is important, so is technical or on-the-job training. If you are a regular user of personal computers, you experience this yourself every time Microsoft or Apple Computer comes out with a new operating system—you have to train yourself in the new ways in which these programs are used. In a similar fashion, there are continuous updates of many types of specific IT technology, such as network routing systems, updated computer languages, communication protocols, and database systems. Training in the use of these is usually obtained through attending educational programs lasting a few weeks or months, with a certificate being issued at the successful completion of them. Employers often look for very specific experience in certain languages, operating systems, or types of computer applications.

ENERGY AND THE ENVIRONMENT

Energy has returned to the top of the list as a social and business concern around the world. People who were present during the previous energy crisis, in the mid to late 1970s, can see a lot of similarities. One of the strongest similarities is how business and academia are responding to the current crisis by developing new technology.

The cause of the current energy crisis is mostly the same as the previous one: the world price of petroleum, the most desired fossil fuel for transportation fuels such as gasoline and jet fuel. The more-than-tripling of the price of crude oil from 2003 to 2006 is adding stress to the automobile, aviation, and shipping industries and generating inflationary pressure that could affect how national economies perform. Because petroleum and natural gas are often used for the same purposes (power generation and home heating), they are linked economically, so a price increase in one raises demand and then prices for the other. Finally, because both fuels are used to generate electricity (along with other sources, such as coal and hydropower), electricity costs are on the rise as well.

A significant difference between the energy crisis of the 1970s and that of the early twenty-first century is the sharper focus on how energy production and use affect the environment—especially with regard to global warming. In fact, the environmental effects of energy and power generation have been present all along; one of the oldest forms of environmental science and engineering was to minimize the air pollution caused by burning coal in cities about a century ago. Since then, highly technological solutions to air pollution have been developed, such as precipitating the dusts and particles present in exhaust gases, or removing sulfur (the source of acid rain) from coal prior to its combustion. The industrial activities necessary to power production—such as building dams, digging mines, and drilling wells—can have a dramatic effect on the environment as well, and technological measures have been adopted to minimize these effects.

However, the problem of global warming takes the energy topic in an entirely new direction. The evidence is now clear that civilization's use of fossil fuels is affecting the global environment. Whether it is possible to reverse these effects—and whether reversing them would reduce the degree of warming that our planet will experience over the next century—is being hotly debated in Washington, Ottawa, other national capitals, and the United Nations.

One near-term result of the global warming debate is the revival of a different form of energy production whose environmental effects had caused it to fall into disfavor: nuclear power. This revival is another example of how energy and environmental issues are intertwined. Nuclear power plants do not produce carbon dioxide or other greenhouse gases linked to global warming. They also do not require the damming of rivers or carving up mountains to extract fuel. However, because of high costs and a very reasonable fear over the effects of radioactive contamination (as seen dramatically at the Chernobyl reactor explosion in the Ukraine in 1986), as well as the continuing problem of nuclear waste disposal, no new nuclear power plants have been built in the United States in decades. In other parts of the world, some nations have decided to end their nuclear power programs, but others have intensified their commitment to developing nuclear power.

HIGH-TECH ENERGY

Research into new forms of energy production has never ceased, primarily because this application possesses one of the hallmarks of high tech—the opportunity to rapidly revolutionize a field of economic activity. Research goes on steadily to provide incremental improvements to energy production; one example is the combined cycle power plant, which uses the energy released by combustion both to generate power and to generate heat (some cities, especially in Europe, have what is known as district heating, where the heat left over after generating electricity can be used in offices and apartment buildings).

Another example of energy research is the on-again, off-again effort to improve the fuel efficiency of automobiles. As fans of high-performance cars know, there is a tradeoff between the performance of an automobile engine and its fuel efficiency. But there have been many efforts to incrementally improve fuel efficiency without sacrificing power; currently, with the price of automobile fuel near a record high, these improvements help sell more-efficient cars and trucks.

Revolutionary changes in energy technology, though, might break the performance/efficiency conundrum. Research focuses on using fuel cells (which combine combustion with electricity generation), hydrogen as a fuel, and all-electric vehicles. Some entrepreneurs are garnering media attention through the use of waste food oils to produce biodiesel fuel as an alternative to petroleum-based fuels, but this is at best an interesting fringe activity, since the volume of food oil that would be needed to displace a significant amount of petroleum would vastly outstrip current production capacity.

Another promising avenue of research is photovoltaics—converting sunlight directly into electricity. Photovoltaic technology is already commercial for specialized applications, such as remote communication posts, and it is being used in a number of showcase high-efficiency buildings. The production techniques for photovoltaics are based on those used to produce microelectronic chips. Although the capital cost of a photovoltaic power plant still compares unfavorably with conventional power generation, improving technology combined with rising energy costs may bring the economic crossover—the point at which the technology becomes economically comparable to other sources of power—nearer.

A truly "wow" research topic in energy generation was the supposed discovery, in 1989, of what was called cold fusion. Fusion energy—the opposite of nuclear fission in nuclear power—is typically an extremely high-temperature process. Two chemists announced in 1989 that they had experimental results indicating that they had succeeded in conducting a hydrogen-into-helium fusion process that seemed to be a net energy producer; however, the changes in process conditions that they measured were extremely small, and it is unclear to this day whether their results were simply experimental error. Still, other researchers continue experimentation in this area.

These examples—and many others—indicate the magical power of energy research. Although the physical laws of thermodynamics and nuclear energy are well established, there often seems to be a radical shift in the tradeoffs between energy production, capital cost of equipment, and waste or pollution generated just around the corner. In the early days of nuclear power, several utility executives were fond of saying that once the kinks in nuclear power were worked out, electricity would be "too cheap to meter" (to charge a price for). As has been seen in the intervening decades, those kinks never quite got worked out. Similarly, there is a concern that the current emphasis on ethanol from crops will exhaust soils and create water pollution in the form of fertilizer runoff, and in fact is only marginally a net energy production technique because of the fossil fuels and energy needed to produce ethanol.

Another group of high-tech applications is being developed for energy conservation, in the form of better types of insulation for structures, capturing more of the energy wasted or consumed during power production, or developing devices that can accomplish an activity (say, illumination) with dramatically lower power consumption.

ENERGY WORKERS

In terms of the types of expertise needed, the following are the common elements of energy production and conservation:

- **Physics.** Physicists specializing in thermodynamics and nuclear physics are most needed.
- **Materials science.** Improved materials are needed in photovoltaics, electricity storage devices like batteries, and high-efficiency heat insulators, among other applications.
- **Process technology.** This is the province of chemical and mechanical engineers and chemists, and determines the steps needed for processes like ethanol production, petroleum refining, or coal conversion.
- **Energy engineering.** This is a specialized area of engineering having to do with the development of power systems for buildings or vehicles, and has an emphasis on energy efficiency.

This list implies that physicists, chemists, and chemical, mechanical, and energy engineers are in demand. For doctoral-level research, job demand is fairly strong, supported, in part, by increased funding for energy research by the U.S. Department of Energy, among other agencies. There is also a small amount of private investment by utilities, petroleum companies, vehicle manufacturers, and venture capital firms.

ENVIRONMENTAL HIGH TECH

Many scientists and engineers are highly motivated, personally, to try to develop technologies that preserve the environment. Recent examples include ways to recycle municipal waste products into reusable materials; methods to reduce the quantity of water consumed by households or farms; skillful adaptation of specialized plants that can naturally clean up polluted streams; and development of appropriate technology for underdeveloped nations so that they can have the benefits of cleaner air, water, or soil without the use of complex mechanized processes such as would be adopted in the developed world.

The great difficulty of environmental work, as currently practiced, is what environmental ecologist Garrett Hardin called "the tragedy of the commons." A commons is a term that used to refer to pastureland commonly held by a community; each farmer or cowherd could make use of it. But in most cases, the farmers or herders had an incentive to maximize their use of the commons and minimize their responsibility for taking care of it. In short order, the commons becomes overused, worn out, and polluted. Primitive societies handled this simply by moving their community to another area and restarting; modern societies do not have this luxury.

In the modern context, private industry likes the opportunity to dig resources out of the ground or to make use of the water flowing in rivers, but the incentive to take care of the resources, or to restore them after use, is dictated only by governmental regulation—there is only rarely an economic incentive to do so. In a similar fashion, consumers want to have the best value for the products (food, clothing, houses) they buy, but don't want to pay more for these things to cover the cost of environmentally responsible production methods unless it is mandated to do so. In short, environmentalism doesn't make money, which forces support of environmental preservation to be funded by governments. And although numerous surveys in the United States have shown that the populace supports environmental preservation and improvement, government funding based on that desire has trended downward in recent years.

There is evidence of change. Although the economic benefits are still unclear, more people are buying hybrid electricity and fuel–based automobiles. There is also heightened interest in "green" or environmentally friendly products, which tend to cost more than conventionally produced ones.

In terms of careers that have an environmental emphasis, nearly every line of scientific or engineering work can apply; the individual makes a choice to do work with companies that have environmental projects. Most branches of engineering have an environmental component; there is also the specific branch called environmental engineering, which is mostly concerned with minimizing air, water, and soil pollution through such technologies as wastewater treatment, air pollution control devices, and waste disposal practices. The life sciences have a clear role to play in sustaining or remediating ecosystems in forests, estuaries, rivers, lakes, and shorelines, as well as improving practices in agriculture.

THREE

The High-Tech Career Paths

Both in the United States and in Canada the importance of science and technology to economic growth is now widely recognized. Universities like the Massachusetts Institute of Technology or McGill University are held as national treasures. And while the typical person relates science and high technology to such common goods as DVD players or personal computers, business managers and government officials recognize that the fountainhead of these technologies is research by scientists and engineers with no commercial purpose in mind—pure research in mathematics, astronomy, physics, biology, and the other sciences.

The previous section provided a survey of the industries and research organizations that deliver new technologies to the marketplace or to the laboratory. This section will examine the fields of academic study that prepare the student for entering those high-tech organizations.

High technology, as previously stated, is dominated by science and engineering graduates. The leading edge of technology—R&D—is often carried out by Ph.D. scientists and engineers. The workers who apply high technology, by installing a computer system in an office or designing a new pollution-control system, for example, usually have a bachelor's or sometimes a master's degree. There are many exceptions to these rules of thumb; one prominent exception is that often a liberal arts graduate, or even a high school graduate, can participate in high technology development.

In this section we'll look at the major groupings of scientific, engineering, and technological college majors that can open the door to a high-tech career. We'll also look at the nontechnical programs that educate members of important secondary professions in high-tech organizations. Keep in mind that the high-tech field is multidisciplinary. More and more, the academic disciplines that one can study as an undergraduate are leaving major gaps in the knowledge needed to solve new types of problems. It is only when experts from a variety of disciplines gather and pool their collective knowledge that solutions appear.

For the individual scientist or engineer, this multidisciplinary need makes it desirable to study in a variety of programs while a student or to explore such options as the double major or the combination of one type of undergraduate degree with a master's degree or Ph.D. in another field. Keep an open mind about the exact major you want to undertake in college and the options you have along the way to graduation.

It is worthwhile to pause a moment before jumping into descriptions of all the professions and academic disciplines in the following pages to consider scientific R&D in general terms. There are many common elements to high-tech work that nearly all of its participants share, and some differences.

The first element to consider is, what is the *R* in R&D, and what is the *D*? Broadly speaking, *research* refers to pure research—done with no specific commercial intention, while *development* refers to research with a commercial intention, either to create or to improve a product. The discovery that an electric current creates a magnetic field was the product of research; the invention of the electric motor, which uses this magnetic effect, was development. Research and development go together because of a springboard effect that they produce: new research leads to new development; new development leads to new research. It used to be a pretty reliable generalization that pure research was done primarily at universities and some government laboratories, while development occurred in the labs of industrial concerns. But today there are strong linkages between academic and industrial scientific work. Many undergraduate science or engineering students, if they take a lab job while at school, may find that they are working on a project sponsored by an industrial company.

One of the fundamental aspects of scientific endeavors is that new knowledge of how the world works is drawn from the evidence that researchers gather. In some cases, this evidence is derived from experiments; in others, from observations of the natural world. The first of these is called inductive reasoning, meaning that you can generalize about how something works in one test to how the same phenomenon functions throughout the known universe. Electricity coursing through a lightbulb in Kansas, for example, will cause the same illumination as it would in China.

The second form of research requires the scientist or engineer to make deductions from evidence found where it is observable. Police detectives use the same reasoning: gathering evidence, making assumptions about what that evidence proves, and then looking for more information that will confirm those assumptions. If wheat in Iowa is dying from a mysterious ailment that causes its leaves to turn black, and it is found that a new infectious organism has been discovered in Alberta, Canada, that causes wheat leaves to blacken, it is not unreasonable to assume that the same organism is infecting Iowa wheat and then to perform tests to isolate it.

Both these forms of research require patient, careful analysis of the observations made during testing or surveying in the field. Careful notes are taken, and this record is reviewed over and over to discover answers. This is the main reason that much scientific progress occurs when a new type of analytical instrument is developed. With the instrument, scientists are able to make observations of things that were unknown previously. It is as if a blind person is now suddenly able to see and can make comparisons between what was only felt in the past and what can now be seen.

Another common aspect of R&D today is that it is collaborative, meaning that many different researchers share in the advances that go on in a field. Sometimes this collaboration is performed actively with researchers sharing data and coordinating their efforts. More often it is accomplished by the pooling of knowledge that occurs when scientists write papers or give lectures. The number of scientific journals has exploded in recent decades, with hundreds of new publications in many languages devoted to increasingly specialized areas of science. One of the challenges of modern research is simply to keep up with this flood of information. More than once it has happened that a discovery made by one researcher was already common knowledge to another; the two were simply reading different scientific journals.

A third aspect of R&D today is that it is increasingly being sponsored by private industry. This is true throughout much of the industrialized world, both in North America and abroad. One of the differences of private research from any other type is that sometimes the researcher doesn't want to share the information with other researchers. The usual reason is that the industrial sponsor of that research wants to profit from it by using the new knowledge to make a saleable product. Even when research is carried out among college professors, there are occasions when some of the results are kept from the public because of industrial sponsorship.

Weighing against this trend is the rising cost and difficulty of making truly useful, truly revolutionary research happen. Not only are various industrial manufacturers sharing in the cost of research, entire nations are, as is happening with many of the satellite launches made in recent years or with the huge atomic particle accelerators physicists use. R&D is a competitive feature of modern economies, but there are more and more cases where it makes sense for nations to share the results so that everyone benefits.

The primary difference between research and development comes into play when research sponsors seek to turn a discovery into a commercial reality. This is when the questions of the cost of materials or the size of a potential market must be assessed before a decision to go forward is made. It is often the source of friction between scientists and technologists and the business managers who have paid for the research to be conducted. The researchers believe that they have conceived an idea that will broadly benefit humanity; the business manager questions whether anyone will buy the product. There are legions of stories about gross underestimations of the commercial potential of a product; in the early days of computer development at IBM, for example, it was believed that there would be only a handful of customers for computers, primarily governments, and so the entire enterprise was questionable. Conversely, there have been many overestimates as well; about a decade ago, Motorola Co. made a billion-dollar bet on a satellite-based telephone communications system called Iridium, which never became a commercial success (there are still some such communication systems in place, but the market remains relatively small). Pharmaceutical companies routinely commit hundreds of millions of dollars to develop and test a new product, only to see it fail in a late testing stage.

This friction between scientific concepts and commercial realities is a source of endless frustration, but also endless excitement, in high technology. High-tech workers are willing to undertake the career risks associated with a new, experimental technology, and they are willing to fight for their vision against a chorus of skeptics. The rewards can be enormous.

CHAPTER

11

BIOLOGICAL SCIENCES

Biotechnology, as categorized by the Biotechnology Industry Organization and others, has three parts: therapeutics (pharmaceuticals and other human health measures); agricultural biotechnology, and industrial biotechnology. Therapeutics and medicine, as an educational and career option, will be dealt with in Chapter 15, "Medical Science"; this chapter will deal with agricultural and industrial biotechnology.

Agriculture, of course, is one of the oldest activities of civilization; it's hard to match farming with high tech—but there are plenty of points of interest common to both. Industrial biotechnology is a fairly new concept, which arose as the common elements of a wide range of industrial activities were unified by modern biological science. Today industrial biotechnology is understood to include the cultivation of plants and animals as a source of useful materials, such as construction materials (wood), fibers (wool, cotton), chemicals (lubricants, dyes, solvents), and, most prominently today, energy. There is a dramatic trend going on in America's agricultural heartland as corn and other crops are being harvested to be converted into motor fuel (gasohol) and as energy producers are looking to biomass as an alternative to fossil fuels.

The traditional conceptions of these industries have been as animal husbandry, forest products, textiles, and so on. In the laboratories of these industries, however, the nature of the work is becoming very similar, based on the breakthrough discoveries in genetics and molecular biology.

A fourth area of interest to the biological sciences is the effects of technology on the natural environment. Ecology is a formal academic discipline within academic biology departments, and while there are relatively few businesses that employ ecologists, this body of knowledge is very important to environmental protection and conservation. (See also Chapter 10, "Energy and the Environment.")

HISTORY OF THE BIOLOGICAL SCIENCES

While medicine and biology are among the oldest professions and fields of study, it was only in the past two centuries that their study became formalized in collegiate programs. While there were medical schools in Europe after the Renaissance, medical care was as likely to be provided by a midwife or a barber as it was by an academically trained doctor. Medicine has a very colorful, dramatic history, with abrupt changes in the field occurring as new science was developed.

A good example of this is the germ theory of disease that evolved during the nineteenth century. As a result of the development of the microscope (in the century before), scientists were able to study bacteria and other microorganisms in a way never possible before. The work of Louis Pasteur (after whom the pasteurization of milk is named) and others showed that these microbes were the cause of many infectious diseases. Previously, people thought that vapors arising from unhealthful, low-lying regions (which tended to have swampy lands) were the cause. Armed with new understanding, public health officials learned to get pure water or to have existing water boiled and to minimize the contamination of foodstuffs. Epidemics of cholera, malaria, and other fevers faded from the scene.

During the 1800s, too, Charles Darwin made his revolutionary theories about evolution and genetics known by publishing *The Origin of Species*, which attempted to account for the development of new life forms (including humans) over the eons. The understanding of natural selection (which is as much a philosophical statement as a scientific one) as the cause of the wondrous proliferation of life throughout the planet has led to dramatic improvements in understanding how livestock or plants can be upgraded to provide healthier crops and better nutrition for humans. At the same time, Darwin's identification of genetics as the key factor in defining a species set the stage for the research that culminated in the 1950s with the deciphering of DNA as the basic genetic code. This Nobel Prize–winning effort by James Watson and Francis Crick in turn opened up the vista of genetic engineering—the manipulation of DNA and the very definition of living organisms. Modern society and the health-care system are still reacting to these dramatic discoveries.

There were notable advances in agricultural and industrial biotechnology even before the modern genetic revolution. In the 1950s through 1970s, a "green revolution" occurred in the cultivation of rice and other grains when agricultural biotechnologists bred drought- and pest-resistant plants whose seeds could be used to dramatically increase the rate of production from a farm. This revolution had a broad impact in the developing world, which lacked the infrastructure of farming equipment that agriculture in the developed world depends on. The green revolution averted a looming food crisis, turning some poor nations that had to import their food into net exporters.

In the modern era vast improvements in scientific instruments, such as the microscope, and improved knowledge of chemistry, physics, and mathematics have built a strong scientific basis to biology. There are new specialties evolving in the field, such as molecular biology, which accept that the principles of living organisms can be explained on the basis of chemical interactions.

With traditional agricultural and industrial biotech practices, workers have been accustomed to receiving harvested products and then performing a variety of manufacturing steps on them, such as curing wood, weaving fibers, or grinding seeds to recover oils and other ingredients. Now there is another component: manipulating the genetic makeup of life forms to emphasize a greater concentration of certain components or to reduce the presence of other components. Livestock that is a source of meat products, for example, can be bred to be lean (lower in fat content). More recently, biotech companies have developed pest-resistant crops by manipulating the genetics of corn and other grains to produce a natural pesticide.

BIOLOGISTS

Biologists work in laboratories, conducting experiments in which, for example, cells are broken apart and the bits of genetic material are collected and then analyzed. Over the years, methods have been established to alter this genetic material—to splice genes from one species into the DNA of another. The product of this gene splicing can then be reinserted back into another living cell, and as that cell reproduces and divides, organisms are created that have a new genetic makeup. Once enough of the cells have been grown, they can be collected in a vessel and manipulated to produce desired biochemicals.

For most research applications a doctorate is highly desirable. The laboratory work is similar to what goes on in college laboratories or even, in a much more sophisticated way, high school laboratories. The main differences, aside from the greater complexity of college-level or research laboratory work, are the access to expensive, sophisticated analytical instruments and the greater use of computers to arrange and then analyze experimental results. Biological research doesn't go on only in the laboratory; many scientists spend most of their time in the field, collecting samples of life forms and studying the patterns of living systems in different environments. In addition, there is a tremendous network—the largest of any of the sciences—in laboratories and research stations sponsored by hospitals, pharmaceutical companies, government, academic institutions, and private research facilities.

Once a set of experiments has been performed and new results successfully obtained, the scientist may publish an article or give a lecture on the subject announcing the findings. At the same time, patent lawyers may be contacted to protect the technology by obtaining patents from government organizations such as the U.S. Patent Office.

Agricultural and industrial biotechnology have their critics, who are concerned that some genetic manipulations could propagate throughout the natural environment, displacing the natural network of plants and animals. Industry has responded by undertaking measures to limit the propagation of new life forms outside the laboratory and by restricting access to locations where genetically manipulated life forms are grown. The proponents' counterargument is that modern biotechnology merely speeds up what has been done for centuries by farmers and others in terms of breeding plants and animals for desired properties. The regulation of agricultural and industrial biotechnology remains an area of concern for governments and environmental organizations.

EDUCATION

Much of biological education is the assimilation of large numbers of facts. Students study basic chemistry and introductory biology, which familiarize them with the processes of biological research. Then a broad variety of specialized courses can be taken that reflect the great number of disciplines under the biology banner. Along the way, the student learns details of the wondrous variety of life, from the biochemicals that make it up to the many organs and systems of life forms to the variety of species of plant and animal life.

In upper-level classes, and especially in graduate school, the many subdisciplines of biology become apparent. Practically every life form has a body of knowledge associated with it that the student can choose to study. Here is a partial list:

- **Biochemistry.** The study of the chemical basis of life.
- **Molecular biology.** The study of the structure and function of biochemicals and genetic matter in cells.
- **Physiology.** The study of the structural composition of life forms.
- **Genetics.** The study of reproduction and inherited traits.
- **Ecology.** The study of the interactions of living things with each other and with the environment.

It is also possible to specialize in a distinct family of living things such as entomology (insects), ornithology (birds), botany (plants), zoology (all animals), ichthyology (fish), and herpetology (reptiles). The idea of research in entomology, to take one example, might strike one at first as a rather boring process of chasing butterflies across the fields. But to demonstrate how high technology intrudes even here, consider that chemical companies seeking to develop new pesticides depend on entomologists to reveal how insect species survive and how they might be safely controlled. Entomology has also become important in many environmental applications, especially where rare species are threatened by human encroachment.

Modern genetics and molecular biology have made some aspects of the study of individual species or families less significant; the thinking is that the study of a species itself is less important than how that species relates to other forms of life. This is some of the logic behind an evolving new field called bioinformatics, which is the structured, computerized analysis and comparison of biological data. At this time, in the high-tech arena, bioinformatics looks to be a useful route to discoveries such as new biochemical pathways to medication or disease treatment. Species-specific work will continue to be important for occupations like wildlife conservation or restoration.

With this diverse array of specialties, it's no wonder that more than 25 percent of biologists go on to graduate school, in addition to the thousands who head for the nation's medical schools. A great distinction is made among medical researchers between those who perform clinical work, meaning that they deal regularly with patients, and those who do not. There are plenty of doctoral-level researchers working on ways to heal illnesses or injuries of humans who practically never work with an actual patient. Rather, they work on samples of cells, or even on a few vials of some biochemical drawn from tissues of human patients or from organisms (such as bacteria or viruses) that infect humans.

Biological high-tech work is not reserved only for the doctoral-level graduate, of course. Those with bachelor's degrees do important developmental work in industrial production of foods and medicines. In addition, bachelor's degree holders are eligible for many positions in the regulation of medical and food-production technologies, which is usually carried out by government-employed inspectors. Finally, there are numerous positions at laboratories in hospitals or clinics, pharmaceutical companies, food producers, and at colleges or privately sponsored research organizations where tests and diagnostic procedures are carried out. This work is very demanding, but also very specialized, featuring technicians who concentrate on the operation of one type of instrument or one type of test. As with research work generally, this work requires careful, patient evaluation of test procedures and results.

12

CHEMICAL ENGINEERING

If you think of engineering generally as the application of scientific principles to manufacturing or construction problems, then chemical engineering is the application of the principles of chemistry to those same problems. Where a chemist makes a discovery by creating a reaction that combines one raw material with another to produce some third chemical, the chemical engineer reaches a goal when that reaction can be carried out in tonnage quantities, using vessels that contain thousands of gallons, at a large, modern chemical manufacturing facility.

Chemical engineering is one of the smaller, more specialized engineering disciplines, but one that has attracted a substantial number of graduates in recent years. The largest fraction of chemical engineering graduates are employed by the chemical industry, but the nature of the chemical engineering education also makes its graduates attractive to a broad variety of employers, including aerospace and automotive firms, electronics manufacturers, oil and mineral producers, and agriculture and forestry products companies. There are about thirty-one thousand practicing chemical engineers in the United States, according to data from the Bureau of Labor Statistics, and almost six thousand Canadian chemical engineers, according to Canadian census data.

ROOTS OF CHEMICAL ENGINEERING

Chemical engineering arose late in the nineteenth century as the chemical industry became an international power in North America. Part of the driving force was advances in processing mineral ores and forest products; another was the development of commercially useful materials from coal by-products (the first hydrocarbon chemicals of industrial interest). Coal-derived chemicals, although they still exist, have been broadly supplanted by petrochemicals refined from petroleum.

A key concept that arose early in this century in the teaching of chemical engineering is that of the unit operation. Unit operations are a way of rigorously defining such common chemical manufacturing steps as evaporation, distillation, mixing, refining, and reacting. A variety of mathematical descriptions were written about each unit operation, and the equipment and procedures required to improve the efficiency of that operation were then devised. In Europe, on the other hand, the model of chemical manufacturing still very much followed the principles of a chemistry laboratory, but scaled up (as the term is used in the business) to a very large size.

In the 1920s developments in North American chemical engineering helped increase the supply of petroleum-based fuels for the booming automobile business. In the 1930s many of the original plastics and polymeric materials that are so common today were commercialized: nylon, polyethylene and polypropylene (used in packaging), polyvinyl chloride (used in plastic pipes), and others. Chlorofluorocarbons, the chemicals now of great concern because of the damage they do to the ozone layer of the atmosphere, originated at this time as a miraculously helpful compound that replaced toxic or flammable materials in domestic refrigerators. (And chemical engineers later helped develop the alternatives, known as hydrofluorocarbons.)

In the 1940s chemical engineers helped devise ways to mass-produce penicillin, the newly developed antibiotic that saved the lives of so many wounded soldiers, and synthetic rubber to replace supplies of natural rubber cut off from the Far East. Late in World War II, chemical engineering expertise was essential in helping to produce sufficient quantities of radioactive materials for the first atomic weapons, which were used in Japan in 1945 to bring the war to an end.

In the 1950s and 1960s North American economies boomed as a consumer-oriented society was created. Vast new quantities of construction materials were required—from plastics for packaging and consumer goods to fuels for the automotive and airline industries. The 1950s are remembered now as the time when synthetics took hold in the minds of consumers as the latest, best products; later, as the environmental problems of chemical production became clearer, synthetic became a synonym for shoddy merchandise—although the quantity of synthetics produced has hardly declined.

THE ENVIRONMENT AND CHEMICAL ENGINEERING

Environmental problems have been closely associated with the chemical industry since the 1960s. Many observers date the connection to the 1962 publication of *Silent Spring* by marine biologist Rachel Carson, who brought national attention to the fact that widespread use of petrochemical-based pesticides (especially the compound known as DDT) was destroying wildlife. In defense of chemical engineering, it can truly be said that chemical engineers were producing materials that society wanted, according to standards that were acceptable at the time. However, those products and standards have left a legacy of pollution and environmental damage that the entire world is still contending with today.

Chemical engineering has undergone something of a revolution in recent years as the seriousness of the environmental issues confronting society has become clear. Today, in fact, chemical engineering is playing an instrumental role in cleaning up past pollution and in preventing further environmental damage. Acid rain—an issue of concern to both the United States and Canada—is minimized when utilities or factories that burn coal or other sulfur-laden materials control the output of sulfur byproducts. But to do this, a chemical reactor called a scrubber must be used after the combustion process. The scrubber neutralizes the sulfur compounds, and in some cases allows them to be drawn out as pure sulfur, which is itself a valuable industrial commodity.

CHEMICAL ENGINEERS

Since the first few years of this century, the job market for chemical engineers has been fairly weak. Many of the industries that employ large numbers of chemical engineers, especially petrochemicals and other commodities, have migrated abroad. However, with the explosion of interest in biotechnology, there is considerable room for growth in the profession, in industrial biotechnology in particular (see Chapter 11). Faced with declining interest in industrial chemicals and rising interest in life sciences, many colleges have revamped their chemical engineering curricula to include more biology and bioengineering.

Chemical engineering also supports energy industries, especially petroleum refining. With the jump in crude oil prices during this century, refiners are looking to expand the production of fuels. The growth of alternative fuels, such as those based on corn-derived ethanol and waste oils, is also leading to job opportunities for chemical engineers.

The job functions that chemical engineers fulfill depend on the type of organization at which they are employed. Typically, in manufacturing organizations, chemical engineers are production managers or process engineers. A production engineer works to keep the facility running as it was designed to and oversees the efforts of the production staff. Process engineers do not have everyday responsibility, but rather they work to improve the efficiency, safety, or productivity of a plant by redesigning components or by changing production practices.

Many chemical engineers are employed at engineering/design firms, where they provide design and construction expertise when a client company desires a new chemical plant to be built. Most chemical companies no longer manage their own construction projects; rather, they call in an engineering/design firm. After the preliminary design goals are set between the designer and the client, staffs of engineers specify the various types of equipment needed, lay out the design for the pipes and electrical connections, and write the initial operating procedures. Starting up a chemical plant is not a simple matter of turning a switch; a complicated, multistep process is undertaken, and the steps must be done in the proper order. Once the plant is running, its operation reverts to the production engineers.

Both chemical companies and engineering/design firms employ chemical engineers to develop new chemical products or production methods.

This developmental engineering work requires close coordination with chemists and other researchers. A key tool for the developmental engineer is the pilot plant, which is a reduced-scale version of an actual production facility. Pilot plants can be complex, multimillion-dollar facilities all by themselves. The goal is to provide data on how a full-scale facility should be run. The pilot plant is where the developmental engineers perform much of their experimentation.

EDUCATION

Like other engineers, chemical engineering students begin their education with basic chemistry, physics, and mathematics courses. The mathematics extends through the sophomore year, including advanced calculus, linear algebra, and differential equations. The chemistry continues beyond the introductory courses to organic chemistry, physical chemistry, and possibly biochemistry or biology. Biology courses are important for chemical engineers who intend to pursue a career in the pharmaceutical or food industries.

Chemical engineering courses include the fundamentals of unit operations, thermodynamics and fluid mechanics, and a design course with a title such as project engineering. In this course, the student attempts to draw together principles of good engineering design with principles of economics, resulting in a manufacturing plant that runs profitably. The options that chemical engineering students can pursue include courses in metallurgy or materials engineering, computer science, electronics manufacturing, biotechnology, or environmental engineering design.

At the graduate level students concentrate on an area of importance to a particular industry or pursue a research direction that will ultimately lead to a new understanding of some basic body of knowledge within chemical engineering. Fluid dynamics—the properties of fluids as they pass through pipes into reactors, or through distillation or separation devices—is one such basic area. When the student seeks employment in a particular industry, courses in such topics as petroleum refining, pulp and paper production, pharmaceuticals, microelectronics, and metallurgy can be pursued.

CHEMISTRY

Chemistry tells us a great deal about how the natural world works. It also guides researchers to determine what products can be manufactured. While many specialized industries, such as electronics, metallurgy, ceramics, foods, and pharmaceuticals, have their own technologies and manufacturing methods, all of them depend on chemistry and chemists to provide the fundamental knowledge necessary to design and make products.

Even so, relatively few chemists are involved in actual production—this is usually left to engineering staffs. Rather, the working chemist helps design new products and production methods and maintains checks on the quality of goods that are produced. Nearly every manufacturer has a staff of quality control chemists who monitor factory output; these chemists continually review product quality by running standardized tests for purity, strength, and other criteria.

HISTORY OF CHEMISTRY

In ancient times chemistry was a popular filter through which to philosophize about nature and the universe, but many of the theories about those topics were clouded in mystical beliefs. An example of this was the theory by ancient Greeks and others that all matter was composed of various proportions of earth, water, air, and fire. Still, the ancients were able to develop metals, glass, and ceramics, so the theorizing had some practical effect.

In the Middle Ages what chemical research and teaching there was existed primarily among alchemists. Alchemy is usually associated with magic and mysticism, not science, but in its time some of the most prominent researchers of their era were alchemists. Isaac Newton, the scientist who helped define modern physics, is one example. Alchemists strove to create gold from base matter and to find a compound that would provide eternal life. While neither of these goals was achieved (although modern nuclear physics now makes it possible to create gold from something else), alchemists developed many procedures for conducting research, processing materials, and measuring the effects of chemical reactions.

Modern chemistry began to take shape in Europe in the 1700s as such scientists as the Frenchman Antoine Lavoisier and the Englishman John Dalton developed sound theories about the atomic nature of matter and elementary chemical reactions. In the 1800s the periodic table of the elements was established, and scientists around the world raced to fill out the lists of chemical categories that the periodic table predicted. Also during the 1800s German and English textile manufacturers established programs of developing dyes and textile-treating chemicals; this led to the formalized structure of organic chemistry (the chemistry of carbon compounds). By now, academic programs at leading universities in both the Old and New Worlds were established.

Organic chemicals—initially from coal, later from petroleum—became the driving force of much chemical research in the early 1900s. The first plastics were commercialized, and much of the underlying theory of chemical reactions and structure was established. During the same period, a combination of chemistry and physics research established nuclear physics and began exploring subatomic matter.

In the 1920s and 1930s chemists and chemical engineers paced each other in developing new materials and new ways of manufacturing them. Thus began the reign of synthetics, such as plastics, textiles, and construction materials, that were thought to be better products because they were human-made. Out of the laboratories and factories came nylon, polyethylene, synthetic rubber, latex paints, high-octane gasoline, pesticides, artificial vitamins, food preservatives, and a veritable cornucopia of other products. World War II spurred this growth and also led to the development of atomic power. In the 1950s the rise of the consumer society added momentum to these developments. The invention of the transistor in the early 1950s demonstrated the importance of chemistry in the nascent electronics industry.

During this period, too, a pattern emerged of chemical research sponsored by industrial corporations. DuPont, the large chemical and energy firm, set the pace with an industrial laboratory led by Wallace Carothers. The pattern was to set up a modern laboratory, staff it with doctoral-level chemists, and guide the progress of applied (meaning capable of being commercialized) research. Oil, agricultural, and metals companies followed suit.

In the 1960s a backlash began to develop to the rise of synthetic chemicals. As previously mentioned, the turning point was the publication of *Silent Spring* by marine biologist Rachel Carson. Carson warned against the practice of indiscriminate spraying of pesticides across the countryside, which killed not only their target—mosquitoes and other pests—but also birds, beneficial insects, and other wildlife. Her book ultimately led to a ban on DDT, a common pesticide.

MODERN CHEMISTRY

Chemistry had grown to a rich and diverse field by the 1960s. As chemical knowledge forged ahead in various sectors of manufacturing and agriculture, new fundamental research by chemists opened up yet other fields for chemists' employment, including such areas as analytical chemistry and biochemistry.

Here is a generalized grouping of today's chemistry subdisciplines:

- **Agricultural chemistry.** The study of fertilizers, pesticides, and soil chemistry.
- **Analytical chemistry.** The study of how to develop instruments and ways to measure chemical properties.
- **Biochemistry.** The study of the chemical nature of life.
- **Environmental chemistry.** The study of the interaction of synthetic chemicals in the environment.
- **Food science.** The study of how to improve or alter foodstuffs to develop healthier foods, such as low-fat foods.
- **Geochemistry.** The study of the chemical processes in the earth.
- **Materials science.** The study of the development of new, commercially useful materials.
- **Organic chemistry.** The study of chemicals based on carbon.

- **Physical chemistry.** The study of the atomic and bulk properties of chemicals.
- **Radiochemistry.** The study of the effects of radiation and radioactivity on chemicals (sometimes called nuclear chemistry).

With such a plethora of specializations, it makes sense for many students to go on to graduate school simply to acquire the knowledge necessary to practice effectively in one of these specialties.

CHEMISTS

In industry, chemists function in certain production roles, but are more often involved in quality control, testing, and process engineering. Many chemists, especially those with advanced degrees, perform R&D in the laboratories that manufacturers operate. In government, chemists conduct research and also are called on for regulatory inspections of the safety of manufactured products and the environmental quality of manufacturing processes.

A perfect example of the energy and excitement in chemistry today can be seen by the race to understand the carbon crystal called buckminsterfullerene (see Chapter 5). Buckminsterfullerene, popularly called "buckyballs," is named after 1960s architect Buckminster Fuller, who popularized the geodesic dome as an inexpensive but efficient way to build shelter. The chemical buckyball is a hollow, sphere-like crystal of interconnected carbon atoms. Buckminsterfullerene opened the door to other forms of carbon, such as nanotubes, and accelerated the entire field of nanomaterials, now one of the most rapidly advancing fields of chemistry.

Like chemical engineering (see Chapter 12), chemistry is evolving to focus more on the life sciences. For many years, the development of new pharmaceuticals has been a branch of biochemistry also known as pharmaceutical chemistry. New drugs were developed by chemists figuring out how to produce a complex compound via a multitude of successive chemical reactions. Now, many of these substances can be created in whole or in part via biologic routes, making use of genetically engineered organisms or cells. This creates a demand for chemists adept at working with these forms of life. And, just as some parts of biology have been superseded by bioinformatics (see Chapter 11), there is an evolving branch of chemistry called cheminformatics that seeks to categorize the broad base of chemical knowledge that exists in the specialty areas.

Chemistry is a great gateway college discipline in the sense that undergraduates with this degree are able to venture broadly in professional schooling and careers. Chemistry is a great preparation for medical school. Some chemists combine this technical knowledge with the study of law or public policy; others expand their technical expertise by studying engineering or another science. According to a 2005 report from the American Chemical Society (ACS), the number of chemistry students earning an undergraduate degree will probably remain constant at about ten thousand a year, although the number of chemists earning graduate degrees is expected to continue to decline through the year 2015. Newly graduated chemists in the United States join a profession that currently has around eighty-five thousand workers, according to the U.S. Bureau of Labor Statistics.

Also according to the ACS, just more than half of all chemists work in manufacturing, 19 percent work in teaching and research, about 15 percent work in nonmanufacturing businesses, and the remainder work in government.

14

COMPUTER SCIENCE AND COMPUTER ENGINEERING

Computer science and computer engineering are the most concentrated computer-related academic disciplines, in that their curricula are strongly focused on the operations of computing systems. But they are by no means the only ones: degrees can be had in information science, information technology, communications, management of information systems (which is often a business-oriented discipline), mathematics, and statistics; even some of the social sciences like sociology can have a strong computational focus.

There are some clear distinctions—and clear overlaps—between computer science and computer engineering. The latter originated as the study of the design and development of actual computers—electronic circuits, input/output devices, and the like. Computer engineering is often a department at the engineering school of major universities. Computer science, on the other hand, has generally been part of the arts and sciences division of the school (where chemistry, physics, and other sciences are also taught). Historically, it was the discipline where logics- and math-minded students would learn how to write computer programs.

In recent decades, several technological developments have changed this distinction. For one thing, an increased amount of program code is embedded in the physical structure of computers; thus, computer manufacturers need computer scientists to help develop the machines. For another, computer design, as well as the design of microchips, mechanical structures, and other parts of computers, is increasingly a computer-aided-design (CAD) function. Designers do not start with a clean sheet of paper; they begin with an empty screen inside a CAD program. Finally, ongoing, rapid advances in computer applications (think of cell phones or the controls on home entertainment systems) blur the capabilities of computer hardware and software. Some computational tasks occur because of better micro-electronics; some occur because of new software.

The upshot of all this is that some college campuses have combined computer engineering/computer science departments; some have one or the other, and some have both, but in separate divisions of the university. The availability of one or both types of programs influences the courses available to the student, which in turn affects the range of options for study.

JOB TITLES

With millions of computer specialists at work, there is a broad range of job titles. As categorized by the U.S. Bureau of Labor Statistics, they are grouped as follows:

Computer and hardware engineers
Computer and information scientists/research
Computer programmers
Computer software engineers/applications
Computer software engineers/systems software
Computer support specialists
Computer systems analysts
Database administrators
Network and computer systems administrators
Network systems and data communications analysts

These are mostly professional titles, requiring a college degree; there are hundreds of thousands more data entry clerks or desktop publishers, most of whom do not have college degrees. Job demand for the professional degrees ranges from high to very high, while the data entry jobs are mostly declining.

Specialty areas, in terms of the nature of the work, range broadly between the design and functioning of computer equipment and the applications that are driven by computer technology. One list, published by the Sloan Career Cornerstone Center, includes:

- Algorithms and theory
- Artificial intelligence
- Architecture (computer architecture), parallel computing, and systems
- Bioinformatics and computational biology
- Database and information systems
- Graphics, visualization, and the human-computer interface
- Systems and networking
- Programming languages, formal systems, and software engineering
- Scientific computing

Generally speaking, it is not possible to match a particular type of computer science or engineering degree to one of these specialties; they draw on all types. The Association for Computing Machinery, one of the oldest and broadest professional organizations for computer scientists, has thirty-four special interest groups that range even farther than this list.

Most computer scientists and engineers work in industry or at commercial establishments, but they are also widely dispersed in government agencies, teaching, and research. It also used to be true that the best computing talents gravitated toward the companies that made computers or offered computing services, such as IBM. However, there are a large number of consulting organizations that are hired to install or operate computer systems for other organizations. To some degree, this is where the practice of outsourcing began, as companies realized it would be cheaper to have a contractor operate their computer networks rather than their own staffs. Then, as remote networking of computer systems became prevalent—driven by the Internet and new telecommunications capabilities—the idea of hosted or managed services arose, by which an enterprise information system was owned and operated by a contractor and the customer simply logged on to a computer account to run a program or to retrieve data. A remarkable feature of today's Internet is that organizations such as Yahoo!, Google, Microsoft Network, or AOL run enormous server farms of computers that host and display website data to anyone on the Internet, and most of the time, the service is free. (The owners of websites do pay for the privilege of having their information available on the Web, but many of them, in turn, offer free hosting services.)

OUTLOOK

Computing and information services are, arguably, the heart of high tech. The capabilities offered by modern information systems are the foundation of much of the research and development that drives high tech. The downside, if it can be called that, of the field is that employers routinely go through dramatic upswings and downturns in employment and in the types of jobs they offer. The workers who succeed in this field are continually renewing themselves with additional training, adapting to newer information products as they become available, and are willing to endure employment instability.

CHAPTER 15

MEDICAL SCIENCE

Medicine and high tech have an uncomfortable relationship with each other. Many patients complain of the impersonality of how modern health care is performed: tests are run, results are analyzed, a procedure or medication regimen is carried out, and the patient is bounced out of the hospital or doctor's office and told to check back in a couple of weeks. Medical doctors themselves are ambivalent about technology; they are eager to apply it when it works, but they also pride themselves on their empathy and worry about the challenges represented by traditional or alternative medicine as treatment for illness. When it comes to the welfare of our own bodies, many of us are equally ambivalent; we want the latest technology, but we have an emotional investment in how we are treated.

Nevertheless, it is indisputable that modern medicine has benefited tremendously from technology. Health-care providers (doctors, psychiatrists, nutritionists, nurses, and counselors) are able to identify the sources of many illnesses very precisely. And while modern medicine is still not the match of some of the scourges of human health—cancer, viral infections, and senility, among others—there has been progress in either eliminating some of them, or in providing treatment that allows a reasonable quality of life to be maintained. New technology is the source of these successes.

Health care is also a big business and one that commands more and more of the resources of the national economy. Like the ambivalence about technology and medicine, the cost of health care is both a testament to the importance we ascribe to health care and a worry over how sustainable the increasing costs are. The past twenty-five years have witnessed a dramatic increase in the business potential that investors see in health care, with public and private investment helping to get the biotechnology industry up on its feet and to fund the development of new instruments, artificial body parts, and, most of all, new pharmaceutical products. This situation drives the growth of medical research occupations.

HISTORY OF MEDICINE

Medicine was a rather disreputable profession until the mid-nineteenth century. Training was disorganized, licensing almost nonexistent. But that didn't matter very much because the body of knowledge with which to provide medical care was limited and, in many cases, simply wrong (for example, the practice of bleeding people to cure them of a disease, or the use of addictive narcotics to treat mental illness). Except for well-established practices such as childbirth, setting broken bones, or sewing up wounds, most of what doctors did was to try to make a patient comfortable while nature took its course. The American Medical Association was founded in 1847, but it took until the early years of the twentieth century to establish educational and licensing procedures that brought some professionalism to the field.

The application of modern scientific practices to medicine by the late 1800s and throughout the twentieth century is easily one of the most dramatic changes in human life. Medical science advanced through the development of specific drugs for illnesses, such as antibiotics and vaccines, and the development of surgical procedures, including such high-profile operations as organ transplants or heart repair. The average life span of Americans has advanced steadily (with a few retrograde years here and there, especially during the world wars) throughout the past century.

Along the way, medical science separated between clinical practice (taking care of patients) and research practice (working in a laboratory to develop new treatments). Teaching hospitals provide training for new doctors, as well as laboratories for research. Medical schools at universities also provide both types of resources and career paths. The U.S. government has built up a vast infrastructure of research organizations and provides billions of dollars for funded research at universities.

In the private sector (excluding, for the moment, private, for-profit hospitals), there are three major sources of medical research: pharmaceutical companies, medical device manufacturers, and biotechnology companies. The first two groups paralleled the growth of medical professions; biotech got going in the 1980s and is now approaching the scale of the pharmaceutical industry. In fact, the differences between the two are fading year by year.

EDUCATION

To be a medical researcher is to make a years-long commitment to education. Most medical scientists have doctorates in specialties such as pharmaceutical science, molecular biology, and epidemiology. In order to perform research involving human patients, the researcher must also be a licensed medical doctor, which entails four years of medical school, plus three or more years working as a resident. Some medical scientists acquire multiple doctoral degrees.

Premed programs at colleges are renowned for their difficulty, leading up to the entrance exams and admission to medical schools, which is a highly competitive process. The student seeking an M.D. degree along a path to becoming a medical scientist must be prepared to sustain a high level of academic performance throughout.

The non-M.D. route to medical research can involve a variety of academic programs in biological sciences, chemistry, public health, biomedical engineering, or others; as new areas of research open up new pathways to treatment, new specialties are brought in. These can include nuclear science, genetics, computer science, and psychology.

OUTLOOK

There are nearly six hundred thousand practicing medical doctors in North America today, and in the United States there are about seventy-seven thousand medical scientists. There is some overlap between the two, as many doctors perform research even while they provide clinical care. The U.S. Bureau of Labor Statistics forecasts a growth rate of 24 percent or higher in these professions in the next ten years.

It is hard to distinguish exceptional career opportunities among medical research areas or types of technology, since part of the structure of medical research (at least as it is funded by the National Institutes of Health) is to ensure that all areas of medicine get some level of research funding. Nevertheless, some of the areas that garner more than average attention from funding agencies and private investors include the following:

- **Personalized medicine.** An era of personalized medicine is coming, whereby a treatment regimen will be attuned to the genetic profile of a patient. It has been seen that some medications might be only marginally beneficial across the general range of patients but can be highly effective for those with certain genetic profiles. Expanding this type of treatment will call for an increased understanding of human genetics and their health outcomes.
- **Imaging technologies.** For decades, getting an x-ray was the state of the art in terms of viewing what was going on inside a patient. Now, through the use of other types of radiation or sensing techniques, more precise views of physiological conditions can be examined, including real-time monitoring of, for example, brain processes.
- **Prosthetic devices.** We are growing more accustomed to artificial implants such as heart pacemakers, replacement joints, and organ-assist devices such as kidney dialysis. Down the road are such innovations as the linking of the electrical activity in the brain with computerized controls to provide mobility to patients with spinal or brain injuries.

The biggest, broadest area of advancement has been, and will continue to be, the products of biotechnology and genetic research. Recently, the pipeline of new drugs being evaluated by the U.S. Food and Drug Administration was larger for biotech products than for pharmaceuticals based on chemical synthesis. This will continue, keeping the employment outlook for medical scientists strong.

C H A P T E R

16

ELECTRICAL ENGINEERING

Electrical engineering comprises nearly one-third of all engineering students and roughly that percentage of working engineers. Because computers and electronics—both the product of electrical engineering technology—represent the totality of high technology to many people, this profession offers the most direct entry into high-tech fields.

HISTORY OF ELECTRICAL ENGINEERING

Even though it is the largest engineering discipline, electrical engineering is also one of the youngest. There was hardly any electrical technology to speak of before the 1880s when Thomas Edison's inventions were commercialized. But since then—what changes! Electrical illumination was shortly followed by electrical power (electric motors), telecommunications (telephone and telegraph), entertainment (motion pictures and recordings), and, at the beginning of the twentieth century, radio.

In the 1920s the first television cameras and receivers were invented, but it would be another twenty years before they became commercially available. By this time, so-called radio engineering was a strong profession of its own. It was out of radio technology that most electronic devices were invented. The development of the transistor in the early 1950s spurred the electronics industry forward, and by that time there were more radio engineers than electrical engineers, even though both were working on electrical technology.

The Institute of Electrical Engineers (which represented primarily those involved with electricity generation and with the use of electricity for motors and heavy machinery) merged with the Institute of Radio Engineers in 1963, and the two professions have been identical ever since.

ELECTRICAL ENGINEERS

Even though we are in the midst of rapid technological change wrought by computers and electronics, most observers of the high-tech scene expect even bigger and better advancements in the near future. The power of a computer that occupied an entire room just a generation ago now fits in the palm of one's hand. Today's personal computer has the processing power of a supercomputer of fifteen years ago, and a similar jump can be expected from today's supercomputers to the personal computer a decade or so hence. One of the troublesome communications issues of today— how to fit television, radio, telephony, and data communications over a telecommunications wire so that all can be carried simultaneously—may be solved in the near future by advances in fiber optics.

The driving force for much of this innovation is the still-incredible shrinking power of the semiconductor chip. Fifty years ago, the technical capability to switch an electrical signal on and off required a glass tube almost as big as a coffee cup. Forty years ago, it required a transistor device about as big as a penny. Twenty years ago, sixty-four thousand transistors could be fitted in the space that a single transistor had occupied, and today four billion of them can fit in that space. With each jump in capacity it becomes easier to put electronics into all sorts of machines and devices— even our own bodies—and to provide stored instructions so that some purpose can be achieved.

These instructions—computer programming—remain a part of electrical engineering, although the growth of the computer engineering field as a distinct profession and college discipline has caused much of that work to move away from electrical engineering. Today it is customary for electrical engineers to be primarily concerned with electrical and electronic hardware—the chips, circuit boards, data storage, and communications devices. Computer scientists and engineers, meanwhile, hold primary responsibility for electronic software—the programs and instructions that the hardware carries out. There remain substantial areas of overlap, however.

The growth of the Internet over the past ten years has dramatically affected the shape of communications, media, business transactions, and research. The hardware components of the Internet are the switches, routers, and servers that carry data from source to destination. Today, the data capacity of fiber optic cables and other communications media is roughly adequate to the demand, but significant improvements are being sought in the switching equipment that directs data to its destination. Wide-area high-fidelity (Wi-Fi) wireless networks are increasingly important to Internet traffic and are seeing similar demands for higher speeds and capacities.

Although it is now a smaller part of the electrical engineering profession, power generation, storage, and use remain an important part of electrical engineering work. Electrical utilities are examining new options in generating power from cleaner, less polluting sources. Nuclear power may reemerge as the most viable power-generation option when, and if, the problems of radioactive waste disposal are solved. Nuclear power may also become the technology of choice to reduce the emission of gases that contribute to global warming. The conservation of electricity, through the use of better materials, electronic controls, and more sensible consumption patterns, is an important issue for power engineers today and will remain so in the future. Solar power, wind, water, and other sources of electrical energy will continue to be developed as practical alternatives to large power stations.

EDUCATION

Once the fundamental principles of electricity, magnetism, and light were worked out by physicists and other researchers in the mid-1800s, a world of opportunities opened up for electrical engineers. This pattern is reflected in the education of electrical engineers on college campuses. Introductory courses in physics and mathematics provide the basic tools for working with electricity. The design of electrical circuits, in which components such as resistors, capacitors, and switches are assembled, is the next step. Finally, electronic circuit design is taught, along with complementary subjects such as materials science, computer programming, and computer theory.

Because there is so much technology to master and advances occur so rapidly in the field, it is quite common for electrical engineers to go on to graduate school after obtaining a bachelor's degree. Most electrical engineers, whether with a basic or advanced degree, work in design—figuring out better arrangements of electrical and electronic components to produce commercial products. A strong trend throughout electrical design practice is the incorporation of electronic devices into circuits. Most electrical companies, and all electronics companies, spend heavily on R&D. Many of them support large laboratories where the fundamental properties of new materials can be studied.

Until recently, the needs of the military were a declining trend in electronic development, both for weaponry and for such technical issues as communications and guidance. The post-9/11 world puts a much greater emphasis on communications security, and that translates into better techniques for both physically protecting communication networks and providing better encryption of data being transmitted. Military equipment development also has resumed growing during the past several years.

Like enrollments in computer science and computer engineering, the number of electrical engineering students declined slightly during the last few years of the previous century, but lately it has begun to increase. More than fourteen thousand B.S. degrees were awarded in 2004, according to the National Center for Education Statistics. Employment prospects for electrical engineers remain excellent.

C H A P T E R

17

MECHANICAL ENGINEERING

From the microwave oven in the kitchen to the automobile in the garage to the power station down the road, machines affect every aspect of our daily lives. The mechanical engineering profession has played a major role in making this come about. Today's mechanical engineers are devising new types of robotics and automation techniques, space exploration vehicles, and pollution reduction technologies for power generation and waste disposal.

Mechanical engineering is the second-largest engineering discipline and as such is deeply involved in nearly every type of manufacturing activity and in service industries and government as well. Mechanical engineering has also taken very well to the advent of the computer: much of the design work mechanical engineers perform is carried out on high-powered computers. Nor should it be overlooked that mechanical engineering is a critical technology for the design and manufacture of computers themselves.

ROOTS OF MECHANICAL ENGINEERING

While there were any number of machines and complex structures in ancient and medieval times, mechanical engineering really came into being during the Industrial Revolution in Europe in the first half of the nineteenth century. The development of steam power, which led to steam-powered locomotives and ships and provided a more dependable power source for factories than water wheels, was a key step to this shift.

During the latter half of the nineteenth century, mechanical engineering exploded in North America. The invention of the McCormick mechanical harvester, the repeating rifle, electrical generators, the telegraph, and the telephone were celebrated landmarks of new technology. Inventors like Alexander Graham Bell and Thomas Edison were national heroes. At the end of that century Henry Ford unveiled his gasoline-powered automobile, and the Wright brothers took their epochal flight at Kitty Hawk, North Carolina.

As significant as these new products were, it is equally important that mechanical engineering technology was instrumental in creating the new manufacturing methods that these devices required. The concept of the modern mass-production factory, in which semiskilled workers repeated manufacturing steps very precisely, in as little time as possible, allowed the new inventions to be marketed cheaply. Mass-production technology was so successful that by the 1920s its proponents looked to it as a way of modeling all social behavior. The technocracy movement of that time was a strong effort to bring this about, but was met with disdain by the time the Depression rolled around.

The unifying aspect of most mechanical engineering technology is material objects in motion. Whether the object is a piston inside an automobile engine or the fluttering of an artificial heart valve inside a patient, materials and motion are the key.

In the era after World War II, as the automobile, the jet airplane, and power tools and appliances became common, everyday resources for society, mechanical engineering grew strong and prosperous. By the 1970s, though, it became clear that as successful as manufacturers had been in the United States, they were not keeping up with advances in Japan and Western Europe. New statistical measures of the quality of manufactured goods were called for, and this effort continues today.

MECHANICAL ENGINEERS

In the early 1980s robotics was thought to be one of the highest of high technologies. Planners envisioned factories without a single worker, where robots would produce perfect products without human intervention. This vision has not come to pass, due primarily to the high cost of quality robotic equipment and the inability to program robots to resolve all the technical issues that a typical machine-tool worker has to deal with. Robotics is not dead—it is still a billion-dollar industry. But the initial vision of pervasive automation throughout all of manufacturing has faded to a more realistic view.

This view is quite thrilling all by itself, however. Manufacturers today have become extremely adept at applying microprocessors to all sorts of machinery. There are microchips under the hoods of nearly all new cars, and fly-by-wire aircraft, which use computers to translate the guidance instructions of a pilot into the actual functions of controlling the aircraft, are now commercial.

This process will continue to intensify in coming years. Mechanical engineers are creating ever more sophisticated computer programs to monitor the quality of manufacturing processes and to run them safely and efficiently. These control networks are hooked into a supervisory level of computers, which automatically collect production data, analyze it, and make recommendations on how the process could be improved. At the management level, the data on plant operations is reviewed by yet another set of computers, and business managers make decisions based on inventory level, forecasted production, and production cost data. The use of statistical measures of production quantity and quality has increased dramatically.

There is no question that of all the sectors of the U.S. economy that have been affected by international competition, basic manufacturing has been hardest hit. More and more basic manufactured products—and an increasing number of advanced technology products—are being imported. However, not all is as it seems. The case of the Detroit-based automobile manufacturers is a case in point. While newspaper headlines lament the job cutbacks or shrinking market share, they tend to ignore the reality that most international auto manufacturers now have substantial operations in North America. Roughly one out of five autoworkers in the United States today works for a foreign auto company, and that proportion is expected to increase. Another factor at work in automotive and other types of manufacturing is that the effect of automation is to reduce the number of employees. As part of a longstanding trend, there is less physical labor in manufacturing, and proportionately more technical expertise.

Like electrical engineers (see Chapter 16), mechanical engineers support a substantial amount of military equipment development and manufacture. The Defense Department budget has been growing rapidly in this decade and is likely to continue to grow for several years. This will boost job demand for mechanical engineers.

EDUCATION

Mechanical engineering students take introductory courses in physics, chemistry, and mathematics. These are followed by the mechanical engineering curriculum, which includes such subjects as mechanics, thermodynamics, automation, and control. At the upper-level undergraduate and graduate levels, it is possible to concentrate in courses relating to a specific industry, such as aerospace, power generation, or transportation.

The number of mechanical and aerospace engineering graduates declined during the 1990s, although not as dramatically as the number of electrical engineering graduates. About fifteen thousand students were obtaining degrees in those two specialties in the United States in 2004, and about fifteen hundred in Canada. Job prospects remain good.

PHYSICS

Physics addresses fundamental questions about matter, energy, and the universe. It is true that, armed with a doctorate in physics, one can address these issues. But most physics students stop after obtaining their bachelor's degree, and for these job candidates, careers in more applied fields open up. The most popular fields for physics employment are in electronics, materials science, and medical or scientific instrumentation.

ROOTS OF PHYSICS

Physics has a continuous history from ancient times to today, especially if one includes astronomy (which is taught in conjunction with physics at many universities). In fact, the history of science is very often summed up as the history of physics, at least until this century. Names such as Aristotle, Ptolemy, Isaac Newton, and Albert Einstein are known to every science student.

In ancient times physics was very much a part of philosophy and even religion; people tried to address human curiosity about the universe around them through whatever scientific means were at hand. By the Renaissance, however, physics had taken on a more earthly nature. Realizing that the Earth was not in the center of the solar system, or the universe itself, helped navigators formulate better methods of mapping the sky and of charting the transit of ships across oceans. By the Industrial Revolution of the 1800s the knowledge that Isaac Newton had revealed about matter and energy helped researchers of that time devise better machines. Physics was also instrumental in developing the electromagnetic theory that inventors like Thomas Edison applied to create practical electrical machines.

By the close of the nineteenth century, questions about the atomic nature of matter had led to the discovery of radioactivity and started the march toward the atomic bomb and nuclear energy. This greater understanding of the atom has influenced chemistry, medicine, and materials science, which are dominant themes in high technology today.

PHYSICISTS

Today physics research marches on, as popular as ever, even though it very often deals with seemingly distant topics like the beginning of the universe or the nature of sub-subatomic matter that exists for only a minute fraction of a second before it disintegrates. While there are physicists who work strictly in such noncommercial areas as cosmology and subatomic matter, and there are others who work solely on commercial applications of electronics or materials, very often the two cross over. A development in the commercial arena, such as warm superconductors, leads to new fundamental knowledge about matter. Or a development in astrophysics, such as new knowledge about the nature of the fusion cycle that powers stars, leads to new knowledge in atomic energy.

The big distinction, then, among physicists is not whether the research is commercial or noncommercial (no one can predict which way such research will go), but rather between doctoral-level research and the R&D work that physics majors with only a bachelor's degree will do.

Such baccalaureate physicists fit very nicely into the electronics industry, where highly sophisticated instruments are used to manufacture semiconductor chips and other devices. Sometimes these graduates get involved in R&D, and sometimes they are strictly technical workers responsible for production of commercial products.

Broadly speaking, there are many areas where a knowledge of instrumentation is valuable. An instrument is simply some tool that helps measure physical properties. It can be as simple as a thermometer or as complex as a particle accelerator that generates high-level radiation. The growth in knowledge of new materials science has enabled the production of all sorts of new instruments, including ones that measure atmospheric properties, provide chemical analysis of small amounts of matter, or detect extremely small amounts of valuable biochemicals during biotechnology research.

The pursuit of nanotechnology going on today is another application of physics expertise. Merely to examine nanotech structures requires complex instruments known as atomic force microscopes. To analyze what is being seen and to translate that analysis into potential manufacturing processes or product applications requires the expertise that physicists can have in such areas as quantum effects, electron tunneling, and other atomic physics areas.

Optics and photonics are another high-tech area for which physicists have ready entrée. Most Internet traffic is transmitted by light (photons) rather than electrons (electricity), at least through the main trunk lines; photons are faster, and more photonic signals can be crammed into an optical cable than an equivalent electrical cable. Images and the process of digitization—whether for digital cameras, streaming video on the Internet, the Hubble space telecope, or the use of infrared light sensors for night vision goggles or analysis of heated surfaces (these are just a few of many more examples)—are a dynamic area of research and product development.

EDUCATION

Physics majors at college take plenty of math courses, including math courses that are taught in the physics department. These are followed by courses in atomic theory, astrophysics, and materials science. Solid-state physics is the term that usually describes courses relating to materials science and electronics, and employers will look for such courses in the school record of students they seek to hire into the electronics industry.

Physics is one of the smallest branches of science in terms of numbers of jobs and students. The U.S. Bureau of Labor Statistics counts fifteen thousand jobs in the field, and projects a lower-than-average growth to sixteen thousand by 2014. It is worth noting, however, that many working physicists do not have that term in their job title; instead, it might be materials scientist, optoelectronics engineer, or one of any number of other titles.

PROFESSIONAL AND TRADE ASSOCIATIONS

American Academy of
   Environmental Engineers
130 Holiday Ct., No. 100
Annapolis, MD 21401
(410) 266-3311
aaee.net

American Association of
   Pharmaceutical Scientists
2107 Wilson Blvd., Suite 700
Arlington, VA 22201
(703) 243-2800
aapspharmaceutica.com

American Association for the
   Advancement of Science
1333 H St. NW
Washington, DC 20005
(202) 326-6400
aaas.org

American Ceramic Society
735 Ceramic Place, Suite 100
Westerville, OH 43081
(866) 721-3322
ceramics.org

American Chemical Society
1155 16th St. NW
Washington, DC 20036
(202) 872-4600
acs.org

American Electronics
   Association
601 Pennsylvania Ave.
   NW, Suite 600
Washington, DC 20004
(202) 682-9110
aeanet.org

American Institute of Aeronautics
and Astronautics
370 L'Enfant Promenade SW
Washington, DC 20024
aiaa.org

American Institute of Chemical
Engineers
3 Park Ave.
New York, NY 10016
(212) 591-8100
aiche.org

American Institute of Mining,
Metallurgical and Petroleum
Engineers (AIME)
345 E. 47th St.
New York, NY 10017
(212) 705-7695
aimehq.org

American Institute of Physics
1 Physics Ellipse
College Park, MD 20740-3843
(301) 209-3100
aip.org

American Mathematical Society
201 Charles St.
Providence, RI 02904
(401) 455-4000
ams.org

American Meteorological Society
45 Beacon St.
Boston, MA 02108
(617) 227-2425
ametsoc.org

American Nuclear Society
555 N. Kensington Ave.
La Grange Park, IL 60525
(708) 352-6611
ans.org

American Physical Society
1 Physics Ellipse
College Park, MD 20740-3844
(301) 209-3200
aps.org

American Public Health Association
800 Eye St. NW
Washington, DC 20001
(202) 777-APHA
apha.org

American Society for
Microbiology
1752 N St. NW
Washington, DC 20036
(202) 737-3600
asm.org

American Society of Civil
Engineers
1801 Alexander Bell Dr.
Reston, VA 20191
(703) 295-6300
asce.org

American Society of Mechanical
Engineers
3 Park Ave.
New York, NY 10016
(973) 882-1167
asme.org

ASM International (American
  Society for Metals)
9639 Kinsman Rd.
Metals Park, OH 44073
(440) 338-5151
asminternational.org

Association for Computing
  (ACM)
1515 Broadway
New York, NY 10036
(212) 626-0500
acm.org

Association for Interactive Media
  (AIM)
1301 Connecticut Ave. NW, 5th
  Floor
Washington, DC 20036
(202) 408-0008
interactivehg.org

Biomedical Engineering
  Society
8401 Corporate Dr., Suite 140
Landover, MD 20785-2224
(301) 459-1999
info@bmes.org

Canadian Aeronautics and Space
  Institute
1750 Courtwood Crescent,
  Suite 105
Ottawa, ON K2C 2B5
Canada
(613) 234-0191
casi.ca

Canadian Council of Professional
  Engineers
180 Elgin St., Suite 1100
Ottawa, ON K2P 2K3
Canada
(613) 232-2474
ccpe.ca

Canadian Geotechnical Society
P.O. Box 937
Alliston, ON L9R 1W1
Canada
(705) 434-0916
cgs.ca

Canadian Society for Chemical
  Engineering
1785 Alta Vista Dr.
Ottawa, ON K1G 3Y6
Canada
http://cheminst.ca

Canadian Society for Civil
  Engineering
130 Slater St., Suite 550
Ottawa, ON K1P 6E2
Canada
(613) 232-6252
csce.ca

Canadian Society for Mechanical
  Engineering
1295 Hwy 2 E
Kingston, ON K7L 4V1
Canada
(613) 789-2467
csme-scgm.ca/default.asp

Chemical Institute of Canada
130 Slater St., Suite 550
Ottawa, ON K1P 6E2
Canada
(613) 232-6252
cheminst.ca

Computer and Communications
    Industry Association
666 11th St. NW, Suite 600
Washington, DC 20001
(202) 783-0070
ccianet.org

Engineering Institute of Canada
1295 Hwy 2 E
Kingston, ON K7L 4V1
Canada
(613) 547-5989
eic.-ici.ca

Geological Society of America
3300 Penrose Place
Boulder, CO 80301-9140
(303) 447-2020
geosociety.org

Institute of Electrical and
    Electronics Engineers, Inc.
3 Park Ave., 17th Floor
New York, NY 10016
(212) 419-7900
ieee.org

Institute of Industrial
    Engineers
3577 Parkway Ln., Suite 200
Norcross, GA 30092
(770) 449-0460
iienet2.org

Instrument Society of America
    Education Services
67 Alexander Dr.
P.O. Box 12277
Research Triangle Park, NC 27709
(919) 549-8411
isa.org

International Society for
    Pharmaceutical Engineering
3109 W. Dr. Martin Luther King,
    Jr. Blvd., Suite 250
Tampa, FL 33607
(813) 960-2105
ispe.org

Junior Engineering Technical
    Society (JETS)
1420 King St.
Alexandria, VA 22314-2794
(703) 548-5387
jets.org

Marine Technology Society
5565 Sterrett Place, Suite 108
Columbia, MD 21044
(410) 884-5330
mtsociety.org

The Metallurgical Society
184 Thorn Hill Rd.
Warrendale, PA 15086
(724) 776-9000
tms.org

National Action Council for
 Minorities in Engineering
440 Hamilton Ave., Suite 302
White Plains, NY 10601
(914) 539-4010
nacme.org

National Society of Professional
 Engineers (NSPE)
1420 King St.
Alexandria, VA 22314
(703) 684-2800
nspe.org

Optical Society of America
2010 Massachusetts Ave. NW
Washington, DC 20036
(202) 223-8130
osa.org

Semiconductor Equipment and
 Materials International
3081 Zanker Rd.
San Jose, CA 95134
(408) 943-6900
semi.org

Sloan Career Cornerstone
 Center
(Web only)
Careercornerstone.org

Society for the Advancement of
 Material and Process
 Engineering
1161 Park View Dr., Suite 200
Covina, CA 91722
(626) 331-0616
sampe.org

Society of Automotive
 Engineers
400 Commonwealth Dr.
Warrendale, PA
 15096-0001
(724) 776-4841
sae.org

Society of Manufacturing
 Engineers
One SME Dr.
P.O. Box 930
Dearborn, MI 48121-0930
(313) 271-1500
sme.org

Society of Plastics Engineers
14 Fairfield Dr.
Brookfield, CT 06804-0403
(203) 775-0471
4spe.org

Society of Women
Engineers
230 E. Ohio St., Suite 400
Chicago, IL 60611
(312) 596-5223
swe.org

Software and Information
Industry Association (SIIA)
1090 Vermont Ave. NW
Washington, DC 20005
(202) 289-7442
siia.net